D0175314

The Practitioner-Researcher

Peter Jarvis

The Practitioner-Researcher

Researcher

Developing Theory from Practice

Jossey-Bass Publishers • San Francisco

Jossey-Bass books and products are available through most book-
stores. To contact Jossey-Bass directly, call (888) 378-2537,
fax to (800) 605-2665, or visit our website at www.josseybass.com.
Substantial discounts on bulk quantities of Jossey-Bass books are
available to corporations, professional associations, and other
organizations. For details and discount information, contact the
special sales department at Jossey-Bass.

 Manufactured in the United States of America on Lyons Falls
Turin Book. This paper is acid-free and 100 percent totally
chlorine-free.

Library of Congress Cataloging-in-Publication Data

Jarvis, Peter, date.
    The practitioner-researcher : developing theory from practice /
Peter Jarvis.
      p. cm. — (The Jossey-Bass higher and adult education series)
    Includes bibliographical references and index.
    ISBN 0-7879-3880-7 (cloth)
    1. Research—Methodology. 2. Research—Management. I. Title.
II. Series.
    Q180.55.M4 J37 1998
    001.4'2—ddc21

                              98-25320

FIRST EDITION
HB Printing   10 9 8 7 6 5 4 3 2 1

The Jossey-Bass

Higher and Adult Education Series

Part Four: Practice and Theory

Part Five: Reflections on the Practitioner-Researcher

Preface

Until quite recently, research and theory were found in the domain of the academy, with practice far removed in the workplace. But the distance between research and practice is rapidly fading as the tremendous pace of global and technological change makes the need for continuous learning an inescapable fact of professional life. Today, research is as much a part of the working world as it is a feature of academic preparation, and work-based learning is fast becoming the order of the day. Research is now about seeking, in a most rigorous manner, to understand and create efficient working practice; that is, it is practice-based.

Evidence of this new environment is the little-heralded emergence in recent years of practitioners who undertake research in the workplace. Practitioner-researchers are found among the many practitioners who return to universities or professional schools on a part-time basis, seeking new knowledge and skills and undertaking small-scale research projects as part of their studies. They are also found among those expert practitioners who are frequently asked by management to provide work-based information that management can use to make relevant policy decisions or provide government and other agencies with information about their company.

Practitioner-researchers are a new breed of practitioner, performing a dual role as both practitioners and researchers. But their research is often small-scale and frequently not defined as research by the research community. They are identified as graduate students rather than as experts and practitioners holding down responsible jobs in the wider world, so what they are doing goes largely unnoticed and unrecognized. But practitioner-researchers have arrived, and they are a symbol of the knowledge society.

The global marketplace demands rapid change, which in turn generates the demand for more practitioners to conduct research. The world of work rather than the ivory tower of the university is the new location for a great deal of contemporary research. Career professionals are conducting that research, within their own occupational specialties.

Society has become reflexive and practitioners have become reflective—both reacting to the consequences of previous events. Reflexive society is a social consequence of modernity, and reflective learning is the inevitable outcome for the individual. The combination of rapid social change and reflective practice creates practitioner-researchers.

The Practitioner-Researcher examines the changing world of work and workplace learning. It reconceptualizes theory, arguing that all practitioners generate their own personal theories, and that apparently objective knowledge of traditional theory is no more than information to be learned and experimented with in practice. The book demonstrates that the traditional relationship between theory and practice no longer holds, and it points to a new relationship between them.

Audience

This book is written for all practitioners—be they career professionals, graduate students, or consultants—who undertake research in the professions and the service industries. A wide range of occupations are discussed in the text. It is also written for educators who work with graduate students and practitioner-researchers. It points to a new way of thinking about students: as both research students and collaborative researchers. Some universities are having difficulty making the necessary adjustments to accommodate the reflexive learning society. This book seeks to clarify both how their role in the world is changing and what direction they will almost certainly have to take in the future. The book thus provides researchers and educators with a different way of examining the relationship between practice and theory, one that is relevant to all who have puzzled about this complex relationship or through their actions have helped redefine it.

Content

The Practitioner-Researcher has two main purposes: to highlight and examine the role of the practitioner-researcher and to try to understand more clearly the relationship between practice, practical knowledge, and theory.

It is divided into five parts. The first part examines the emerging role of the practitioner-researcher and notes some of the early ways that educators of professionals changed their initial preparation to overcome the problems they confronted in discussions of the theory-practice relationship. The second part examines the nature of practice, reflective practice, and practical knowledge. Considerable weight is given to the fact that knowledge is now regarded as subjective and practical; this leads to a distinction between knowledge and information.

Types of research that practitioner-researchers are mostly likely to undertake form the basis of the third part: both qualitative and quantitative approaches are discussed. Because of the transitory nature of practice, I argue that research into practice must take the form of qualitative case studies. The use of documentary evidence forms a link between the qualitative and the quantitative. The fourth part reconceptualizes theory, points to the significance of personal theory, and indicates that there is a process from practice to theory—and from theory to practice. Finally, the book looks at the changes that are occurring in the relationship between education and the world of work and calls for a partnership arrangement between higher education and the corporate university.

Background

This book brings together my thinking and work on this subject over many years. My doctoral research was in the sociology of professions, I examined the relationship between ideology and job satisfaction. For a while I taught sociology and sociological theory at the college level and then shifted my attention to working adults—schoolteachers, nurse trainers, and educators from a variety of other professions. An invitation to present a paper at a conference on professionals' acquisition of knowledge started me thinking seriously about the implications of my learning model for work-based learning.

I have been privileged to work with practitioners from a considerable number of professions (such as nurses, midwives, doctors, adult educators, and clergy) in the past few years, and many have been excellent practitioner-researchers. What I have learned from them has reinforced my reading on professions and organizations. However, when I started to write this book, I found that it was becoming abstract and theoretical. The manuscript reviewers Jossey-Bass employed were rightly critical—the book was originally missing some of the crucial elements about which I wanted to write—and I am extremely grateful to them for their insight. Above all, I am tremendously grateful to Gale Erlandson, senior editor for the Jossey-Bass Higher and Adult Education series. She had great confidence in this book, and I can only hope that this manuscript has justified her faith in me. My wife allowed me space and encouraged me to write, even if it meant spending all my spare time imprisoned in my study.

The book is written for practitioner-researchers; I hope that it does justice to the role that they play. In keeping with the philosophy of the book, I urge you to test it out—use what works for you and forget the rest. I hope at least some of the ideas expressed here will prove both useful and relevant.

September 1998   Peter Jarvis
                                                              Guildford, Surrey, England

The Author

Peter Jarvis is professor of continuing education in the School of Educational Studies at the University of Surrey, England. He is also adjunct professor in adult education at the University of Georgia in the United States. In addition, he teaches sociology for the Open University part-time and is a nonexecutive director of the Management Consultancy Business School.

Jarvis earned a bachelor of divinity degree from the University of London (1963), a bachelor of economic arts degree in sociology from the University of Sheffield (1969), a master of social science degree in the sociology of education from the University of Birmingham (1972), a doctor of philosophy degree in the sociology of the professions from the University of Aston (1977), and an honorary doctor of philosophy degree from the University of Helsinki (1997).

Jarvis's work, having sociological and philosophical foundations, has focused mainly on aspects of the education of adults and lifelong learning. He has taught teacher, adult, vocational, and continuing education and has undertaken a variety of research projects, some of which were connected with nurse education. He has been involved in distance education for over twenty-five years. In 1988, he was awarded the Cyril O. Houle World Award for Literature in Adult Education for his book *Adult Learning in the Social Context* (1987). He was also awarded the Comenius Award of the European Society for Voluntary Associations in 1997, and in the same year was inducted into the International Hall of Fame of Adult Education in America. In 1990, he was a Research Fellow of the Japan

Society for the Promotion of Science at the University of Tokyo. He is also a Fellow of the Royal Society of Arts.

Among Jarvis's other publications are *Professional Education* (1983), *Adult and Continuing Education: Theory and Practice* (1983, 1995), *The Sociology of Adult and Continuing Education* (1985), *The Teacher Practitioner in Nursing, Midwifery and Health Visiting* (1985, 1997, with Sheila Gibson), *An International Dictionary of Adult and Continuing Education* (1990, 1998), *Paradoxes of Learning* (1992), *Adult Education and the State* (1994), *Towards the Learning City* (1997, with associates), *Ethics and the Education of Adults in Late Modern Society* (1997), *The Human Resources Development Handbook* (1998, with Pat Hargreaves), and *The Theory and Practice of Learning* (1998, with John Holford and Colin Griffin). He has also edited a number of books, including: *Twentieth Century Thinkers in Adult Education* (1987), *Training Adult Educators in Western Europe* (1991, with Alan Chadwick), *Adult Education: Evolution and Achievements in a Developing Field of Study* (1991, with John Peters and Associates), *Perspectives on Adult Education and Training in Europe* (1992, 1998), and *Adult Education and Theological Interpretations* (1993, with Nicholas Walters). He has published more than 150 papers and chapters in books, and his work has been widely translated.

Jarvis is a founding editor of *The International Journal of Lifelong Education*, has edited two series of books on adult education, and serves on the editorial advisory boards of journals in a number of countries. He is a frequent speaker and lecturer on adult, continuing, and higher education and lifelong learning in many parts of the world.

The Practitioner-Researcher

Part One

Understanding Connections Between Research and Practice

Chapter One

The Practitioner-Researcher

A new phenomenon has emerged in recent years: practitioners in many occupations are undertaking a great deal of their own research. Traditionally, research has been the preserve of academics and scientists who have had the necessary knowledge and skills to conduct research; they have pronounced the results of their undertakings, and practitioners have been expected to abide by and implement their findings. These pronouncements have been incorporated into the profession's body of knowledge, which has then been applied to practice. But things are changing. The idea that theory should be applied to practice is increasingly being recognized as an oversimplification, at the least, and at the most, as false. Many practitioners are now conducting their own research, even though it is not always referred to as such, and much of it does not get incorporated into their profession's body of knowledge.

Among the reasons that things are changing are that research practice itself is undergoing rapid change and few practitioners are actually doing precisely the job for which they were trained; more knowledge is being legitimated pragmatically rather than either logically or empirically; the high status of theory is being questioned; academic qualifications are becoming symbolic of ability, and gaining them is becoming a necessity for career advancement; and scientific management requires more data on which to base decisions. I return to each of these points as the book progresses.

Throughout the book, practitioners who do research are referred to as practitioner-researchers. This role has emerged almost unnoticed despite the fact that in education, Schwab was urging schoolteachers to perform this role in America as early as 1969, and only a few years later Stenhouse (1975) was doing the same in the United Kingdom. But new concepts do not always develop in precisely the way that early thinkers anticipate.

Indeed, many of the practitioners who have become practitioner-researchers do not always regard themselves as such. Students nearing completion of a doctorate and holding full-time jobs tend to define themselves as practitioners, entirely overlooking the research aspects of their activities. Or practitioners may often not be perceived as genuine researchers because they define themselves as both practitioners and students. For many people, research implies being employed by a university or a large private organization, big projects, funding from foundations and other outside sources, research assistants, deadlines for completion of research projects—all the accouterments of traditional ("real") research. But the truth is that far more research goes on in small projects, often unknown to and unrecognized by many people in the professions. Furthermore, the findings of some of these projects never see the light of day—the assumption is that publication is for "real" research conducted under strict scientific standards.

The findings of small-scale research are regarded as anecdotal; they are not scientific in any way, so they are not considered valuable to genuine researchers. But there is a major flaw in this thinking: the experts are not always right, and sometimes the practitioners actually know a lot more than the acclaimed specialists. Lash and Wynne (1992), in their introduction to Beck's *Risk Society*, provide a nice illustration of this:

> When farm workers claimed that herbicides were causing unacceptable health effects, the British Government asked its Pesticides Advisory Committee to investigate. The PAC, composed largely of toxicologists, turned to the scientific literature on laboratory toxicology of the chemical in question. They concluded unequivocally that there was no risk. When the farm workers returned with an

even thicker dossier of cases of medical harm, the PAC dismissed this as merely anecdotal, uncontrolled non-knowledge.

When they were forced by further public objections to return to the question, the PAC again asserted that there was no danger, but this time they added an apparently minor . . . but actually crucial qualification. There was no risk according to the scientific literature, so long as the herbicide was produced under correct conditions and used under correct conditions [pp. 4–5].

But the "correct" conditions were the laboratory, not the farm. We are aware that things like this happen all the time—that decisions are delayed until the "scientific" evidence is discovered, even though ordinary practitioners know from their experience that what they claim is true. Another example might be the so-called Gulf War syndrome, which still awaits the experts' conclusions. The reassurances that we get from the specialists might be as meaningless as they were from the PAC because their reports are prepared under controlled conditions rather than in the world of practice. They have the image of being genuine scientific research, even though their pronouncements may often be no more valid—and often less valid—than the findings of the practitioners.

Who Are the Practitioner-Researchers?

When I imagine the quintessential practitioner-researcher, I envision a nurse teacher who has spent many years working for her master's degree and is now working on her doctorate, who has published some of her findings and who will continue to research her practice when she has received her doctoral degree. She is typical of a large group of professionals who undertake further education and research while they are working.

Many practitioner-researchers are expert practitioners working toward graduate degrees as part-time students. They are expanding in number because of the growing significance of continuing education in recent years. Many part-time master's degree and practitioner doctoral programs now require that students conduct a small research project for their dissertation. In addition, the number of people with research doctorates has grown. Because this is true for nearly all occupations and professions, there are many more practitioner-researchers than there might initially appear to be. Indeed, many occupations are genuinely concerned that any graduate courses taught to their practitioners should be practice-based, and that the dissertations should be grounded in practice.

I have recently been involved in developing a master's degree program in management consultancy. Unlike many degree programs, this one was not designed by the university professors and then offered to the industry—as though the university were preparing the theory and the practice would in some way follow it. This degree program was designed by the industry, with university professors participating in the committees as active members. Significantly, there is a research component—and the practicing management consultants who study for this degree will be using learning materials designed by experienced and practicing management consultants reflecting on and researching their own practice. The very first course in management consultancy at the graduate level is bound to produce even more practitioner-researchers—although this was not its original intention and is not its present goal.

There are also many practitioner-researchers in different occupations and professions who carry out small projects for management in order to provide information for policy decisions. The need for such information has grown as scientific management theories have become more widely implemented. Indeed, to uncover information they require, government and other authorities are sending extremely lengthy questionnaires requiring considerable time and research to employees and organizations they fund. The need for such information is also generating a greater research orientation among practitioners.

Nursing has introduced the idea of "evidence-based practice" (Finch, 1998) ; this might mean that nurses seek externally validated research data, but it can also result in practicing nurses using the results of internally validated evaluations and research projects undertaken by themselves and their colleagues.

Finally, there are others who undertake research to satisfy their own curiosity. These are practitioner-researchers, but they often are not recognized as researchers. They certainly do not have the traditional image of the researcher, and they may not always be in a position to conduct their research in a most satisfactory way, nor do they necessarily meet the stringent demands of some members of the traditional research community. Nevertheless, this does not mean that they should not be viewed as practitioner-researchers, because that is what they are.

The research community defines the epistemologies of research and also controls its image. This is a natural social process, but it takes a long while for traditional images to change and for new conceptions to come to the fore. But it is clear that both the traditional image and the new conception of research are already undergoing change.

The growth in the number of practitioner-researchers has occurred for a number of reasons, including the need for more information for use in decision making at the managerial level, the need to keep abreast of new knowledge and procedures in this information society, and the need for continuing education and upgraded qualifications. But can expert practitioners also become experts in research, or are there some other models that we need to explore?

Playing Two Roles

In the 1980s, I wrote, with a nurse educator, a book that addressed the question of whether it is possible to straddle two professions (Jarvis and Gibson, 1985). We concluded then that it was, although we thought it would prove difficult to keep abreast with the demands of both roles. It is difficult, but now there are lecturer-practitioners in nursing in the United Kingdom. Our book did not trigger this innovation; it simply appeared at an appropriate time.

But as I thought about straddling two roles, I realized that there are many of us who do it much of the time: professors who also practice the professional skills of the occupation that they teach, professors who consult in their own area of specialisms, senior doctors (consultants) who teach their students, managers who are mentors, and so on. Indeed, in teacher education it is becoming increasingly recognized as important that trainers spend time teaching children as well as teaching students. Straddling two occupations is a rather common occurrence—except, it appears on the surface, in research. In point of fact, however, we do have many practitioner-researchers; it is not a new role. But neither was teacher-practitioner new when we wrote that book; it is just that they were not always recognized as such. More significant, they were not defined as teacher-practitioners. Recognition of practitioner-researchers suffers the same failings.

There are some problems with performing two roles simultaneously, especially when the roles are not recognized. Some practitioner-researchers still see themselves strictly as practitioners. It is in practice that they have gained their sense of self-identity. Once they try to see themselves as researchers as well, their own role identity might change, and that might in turn affect the way they perceive and perform their practice role. For example, if their job has changed from being a site for practice only to one for practice and research, they might no longer perform their practice role as they would have had they not been performing the research role.

Performing dual roles also raises ethical issues in that the practitioners are dealing with their colleagues and clients as practitioners. Should they also be using this role to act as researchers? One of my doctoral students, who is researching her own practice as an international health consultant, said that there have been times when she has had to restrict her research in order to pursue the consultancy. For instance, while she was meeting with senior government officials in one of the countries in which she was working, she wanted to ask them research-related questions rather than the ones that were focused on the work that she was doing. She knew that that was not the type of interaction she should be having, even though her clients were aware that she was also researching her practice. When she was able to return to the research, the issues that she has previously wanted to explore no longer occurred quite so naturally as they had in the original practice situation, so the research was slightly artificialized. It does not matter how good her memory was or how willing her clients were to discuss the previous matter; the actual point of practice had passed. But to have pursued her research at an inappropriate time in her practice would not have been moral.

Highlighting the problems of the practitioner-researcher does not mean that the role is not important. Just the opposite is true. Like many occupations, it has its own intrinsic difficulties. It might be claimed, however, that this endeavor to combine two roles into a new one is flying in the face of the demands for continued specialization in order to keep abreast with all the changes in each profession. Most people recognize the need for specialization, but there are times when, say, a sick person needs a generalist doctor rather than a specialist in an unrelated branch of medicine. There are times for specialists and times for generalists—some people will specialize and some will not, and others will continue to combine two different roles successfully. This final group will also help break down traditional boundaries.

In fact, crossing boundaries is quite a common feature in contemporary society. They are often being completely redefined. For instance, the external structures of school education have been questioned by Giroux (1992), who assessed his own previous writing and claimed that his present book "is an attempt to broaden the parameters of how we think about schooling, pedagogy and cultural politics" (p. 2). Similarly, it was reported that because of a lack of skilled graduates in engineering, British Aerospace had decided to create its own university, which would award its own degrees ("Dearth of Engineers," 1997). This has already occurred in the United States, as Eurich (1985) clearly showed. We also know of Motorola University, Disney University, and so on. Thus we see that the boundaries between higher education and the world of work are themselves being redefined. Similarly, we are seeing the boundaries between adult and higher education disappear as more adults return to school to continue their professional education. We are now also seeing the boundaries between research and practice dissolve.

As the boundaries are dismantled, new roles begin to emerge and gain recognition. Practitioner-researchers might also begin to be defined as such and recognized for who they are and what they do. As far as I know, there are few, if any, full-time appointments designated as practitioner-researcher positions, although there are researchers employed to examine practice—not quite the same thing.

It is high time that such a position be considered, but whether there should be such designated roles is another matter as well, because it might well be argued that all practitioners should be practitioner-researchers.

Conclusion

Practitioner-researchers play two roles, and I analyze both in this book. First I examine the practitioners who do research; then I look at practice. After that, I spend some time looking at the implications for practitioner-researchers of the research they can undertake. Next I seek to draw this all together in a section on theory. Finally, I look at the implications of this discussion in terms of both the relationship between theory and practice and the continuing learning of practitioners.

Chapter Two

Educating the Practitioner-Researcher

It seems quite natural to us that new recruits to a profession or occupation should go first to school or university to learn its body of knowledge—its theory—before they enter practice. Indeed, as occupations have professionalized, they have created their own training schools, developed their own body of knowledge, and sought to gain accreditation by academic institutions so that new recruits can have what they considered a proper education and training (Caplow, 1954; Greenwood, 1959; Wilensky, 1964). But why should they not first go into practice in order to learn how to do it, or at least to learn what they need to learn, and then go to university to learn its theory? That does not seem at all obvious to us today, and some might well dismiss it, saying, "That's like the apprenticeship system—it's old-fashioned and out of date." We might belittle the idea of apprenticeship, and it might actually not be beneficial to go into practice first, but perhaps the dichotomy between these two approaches is oversimple. Other approaches to preparation, such as sandwich courses, practicums, and problem-based learning, have already been introduced, and they have implicitly questioned the idea that theory should always precede practice. Finally, periods of probation after having completed the training also suggest that the initial preparation is not regarded as sufficient.

The apprenticeship system might seem old-fashioned, and it is certainly premodern, in the language of contemporary sociology and philosophy. The idea of applying theory to practice indicates that scientific knowledge had become dominant in the West since the Enlightenment—in modernity. But over the past few years, the questioning of the tenets of modernity has been growing, and scholars have written about postmodernity (Lyotard, 1984; Jameson, 1991; Harvey, 1990), late or high modernity (Giddens, 1991), and reflexive modernity (Beck, 1992). The changes we are seeing in the initial preparation of professionals are part of this same process, and the emergence of practitioner-researchers is also an indication that we are entering a new era of late or reflexive modernity. I briefly explore the implications of these changes in the initial preparation of professional practitioners, and then I examine some graduate courses in continuing education.

Initial Preparation

We look here at four approaches to the initial preparation of practitioners: apprenticeship, professional school, sandwich-type courses, and probationary periods.

Apprenticeship

Heidegger (1968) makes an interesting observation about apprenticeship:

> A cabinetmaker's apprentice, someone who is learning to build cabinets and the like, will serve as an example. His learning is not mere practice, to gain facility in the use of tools. Nor does he merely gather knowledge about the customary things he is to build. If he is to become a true cabinetmaker, he makes himself answer and respond above all to the different kinds of wood and to the shapes slumbering in the wood—to wood as it enters into man's dwelling with all the hidden riches of its nature. In fact, this relatedness to wood is what maintains the whole craft. Without that relatedness, this craft will never be anything but empty busywork, [and] any occupation with it will be determined exclusively by business concerns. Every handicraft, all human beings are constantly in that danger. The writing of poetry is no more exempt from it than is thinking.

Whether or not a cabinetmaker's apprentice, while he is learning, will respond to the wood and wooden things depends obviously
on the presence of some teacher who can make the apprentice com-
prehend [pp. 14–15].

Thus the apprentice is not educated in scientific knowledge but
rather looks for the shapes that slumber in the wood, for an awareness of what the wood can become in his hands. Learning to use
the tools is one thing, but being able to produce a beautiful object
from the wood is quite another. Heidegger (1968, p.15) goes on to
make a telling point about teaching the apprentice: he writes,
"Teaching is more difficult than learning because what teaching
calls for is this: to let learn" (p. 15). This idea is very much in accord with our era.

When we see the premodern apprenticeship described in such
a beautiful way, it seems a little more sophisticated than merely
copying the practices of a master craftsperson, or "sitting by Nellie,"
as we say in the United Kingdom. But then the image of apprenticeship was defined by the epistemology of modernity—and
with the emergence of modernity, the pendulum has swung away
from the creative arts, which have become mere skills to be learned.

Going to Professional School.   The modern approach to professional preparation emphasized knowledge, and new recruits were
then expected to learn their theory and go and apply it to their
practice. Theory defined practice and was important because it
emerged as a result of research that was scientific and therefore
right. The theoretician was the legitimator of the correct knowledge (Bauman, 1987) and had a much higher status than the practitioner, who merely applied it.

For many years now, however, voices have been questioning
the relevance of this approach, epitomized by a very common sce-
nario: when the students first go into a practice situation, they are
often told by experienced practitioners, "Forget everything you've
learned in school." When they return to the school, they frequently

complain, "All this stuff we learn here is irrelevant," or "Theory is worthless!" Nearly all express the excitement of being in the practice situation and bemoan how boring and useless it is to learn all this theoretical knowledge. Educators in all professions have experienced this.

Some professors defend their position by claiming, "They haven't learned to apply their theory to practice." They insist that new recruits have got to learn the theory so they can produce best practice. They have also frequently justified themselves by proclaiming that "there is nothing as practical as good theory." But these views are changing.

But we might ask, why did the theorists get such high status? Knowledge, especially scientific knowledge, had become very important, and all the occupations and professions wanted to ground themselves in science. Scientists had high status; practitioners who did not know their theory did not. Practitioners needed to learn more in order to perform better. Theory was so highly esteemed that there was no practical training in some of professions even as late as the 1960s. But this approach was being questioned.

Practicums and Sandwich Courses. As occupations gained professional status, the amount of theory being taught grew and took precedence over the practice; although medicine has always insisted on long periods of training in hospitals during initial preparation, significantly less time was spent with general practitioners and in health centers and community medicine. Other high-status professions, such as the professoriate and the clergy, have included little practical training until recent years (although it might be claimed that one of the traditional routes into the professoriat has been through being a graduate assistant, learning both the skills of researching and, occasionally, teaching—an apprenticeship model).

Schön (1987) records how architecture and other professions use practicums. He defines a practicum as "a setting designed for the task of learning a practice. In a context that approximates a practice world, students learn by doing, although their doing usually falls short of real-world work. . . . The practicum is a virtual world, relatively free of the pressures, distractions, and risks of the real one, to which, nevertheless, it refers" (p. 37). Schön's practicums involved groups of architecture students working together on projects, and he correctly claims that the group forms a learning set that becomes as important to each member as their coach is. The students are clearly involved in a virtual world of work; like the airline pilot in a simulator, the experience is close to the real thing but is not entirely real. In the pilot's case, the experience may not be the same as it would be in an airplane, but in the students' case, there are times when the experience could be authentic.

By contrast, the semiprofessions (teaching and nursing, for example) have always had long periods of internship as part of their initial preparation, providing opportunities of learning how to do the job. For a number of years, I worked in a college of education, preparing schoolteachers. Frequently, we went into the schools where the students were doing internships, practicing teaching in actual classrooms under the guidance of an experienced teacher.

Students were expected to write up and evaluate their lessons, prepare case studies, and seek to learn from practice. They were not merely to ask their mentor to help them—they had to carry out the research themselves.

In the university in which I now teach, we have had for decades a professional practice year in many of our undergraduate programs. Students go into industry, commerce, public service, and the arts for the third year of a four-year full-time degree program. This is the *sandwich course*—a practical year "sandwiched" between years of study. They work in companies on real jobs, take some measure of responsibility under a mentor, and are expected to meet the customers and to be totally involved in the life of the company. Many of the professional-year placements are not in Britain or even in English-speaking countries.

Recently, one student described how he had been placed in the aircraft industry as an engineer in a company that had establishments in Germany and France. His year was spent on design projects mostly in Germany and speaking German but also for a while in France and speaking French. He introduced his presentation to the

University of Surrey in German. He then told us, in English, what projects he had participated in and how the company was going to use his work in its current developments.

During the year, the students are visited on several occasions by a university professor designated to be responsible to the university for their work, and assessment of their work may be undertaken by the company as well as by the university. Indeed, it is often the mentor who sets the assessment project. This approach has many advantages, perhaps the most obvious being that in the year 1996–97, the University of Surrey had the highest percentage employment among its graduating students of any university in the United Kingdom, including Oxford and Cambridge.

In practicums and sandwich courses, students are introduced to both theory and practice together, showing that both are important to the practice situation. In the case of the engineering student, it is important to note that he had acquired a considerable amount of content knowledge (knowledge of the academic disciplines underlying the practice of engineering design) before he undertook his practical placement. During the professional year, however, he learned both a great deal of process knowledge (knowledge about how to be an employee in a multinational aircraft engineering company) and even more content knowledge. For the moment, I want to give these two forms of knowledge another name: content knowledge is *knowledge why*, and process knowledge is *knowledge how*. We return to these terms later in the book.

Even more significant, the engineering student also learned *how to do*. It is important to note that *being able* or *knowing how to do* is logically different from *knowing how*. For instance, I might be able to ride a bicycle, but I cannot provide an aerodynamic explanation of why I remain upright—in other words, I know how to do it, but I do not know how it happens.

Probationary Period. Employing newly qualified entrants to the profession might seem risky, especially if they have had little or no practical experience. Members of the professoriate, for instance, spend a long time in probation before they gain tenure, and many other occupations and professions impose a practical period before they allow certification or the status of a fully employed person. This probationary period is like an apprenticeship, helping the newly qualified practitioners master the arts of practice, learning to do, before final acceptance into the profession. Implicitly, this system also indicates that the relationship between theory and practice is much more complex than had been assumed during the period of modernity.

During their initial preparation, practitioner-researchers might receive some basic introductory courses in research method, and more recently they might have been expected to undertake a small research project, but it would be hard to assert that initial preparation should be about preparing the new recruits to do more than just practice. Major innovations in teaching in recent years, however, have helped to prepare practitioner-researchers.

Changes in the practice of teaching itself have certainly helped foster this development of practitioner research. Teachers and professors now recognize that they are not necessarily teaching the "truth," so they are employing more open-ended teaching methods, group discussions, projects, and so on. As Brookfield (1987) has also highlighted, students are being encouraged to become more critical in their thinking. Bauman (1987), a sociologist, has rightly claimed that now teachers are interpreters rather than legislators of knowledge.

In teacher training, for instance, students have been expected to undertake case studies of children and prepare evaluations of their teaching practice—small pieces of research. In nurse training, students also keep reflective diaries to record the way they have responded to critical incidents and so on. In many professional placements, from teaching to nursing, students write up their projects and keep journals. These approaches are all furthering the development of practitioner-researchers.

The use of the reflective practicum, Schön (1987) notes, is producing a greater research orientation toward practice. "Creation of a reflective practicum calls for a kind of research new to most professional schools: research on the reflection-in-action characteristic of competent practitioners, especially in the intermediate zones of practice, and research on coaching and on learning by doing. Otherwise, the schools will find it difficult to determine how their earlier conceptions of professional knowledge and teaching stand in relation to competences central to practice and the practicum; their efforts to create a reflective practicum may only produce a new version of a dual curriculum in which classroom teaching and practicum have no discernible relation to each other" (p. 171). Schön is certainly correct in the concerns and insights he expresses here, but perhaps he might have extended his analysis even further and shown how the reflective practicum also contains a research orientation in itself, fostering in students an inquiring mind necessary for research.

In a similar way, another innovation in professional preparation that encourages the development of the practitioner-researcher has been problem-based learning. Introduced in medical education by Barrows and Tamblyn (1980), problem-based learning has been used in the initial preparation of practitioners. It is a process of designing a professional curriculum so that students are given practice problems to solve during their coursework. It has now become one way of training new recruits to a profession in which students are encouraged to relate theory to practice. Many different experiments have been attempted in using problem-based learning to prepare new entrants to professions (Boud, 1985; Boud and Feletti, 1991). One of the problems with problem-based learning, however, is that the potential learning situation is created by a problem rather than a success, and there is a sense in which success is as much a problem as failure. Even so, solving a problem can be a research process.

All of these innovations in professional preparation are promoting in students the kinds of inquiring minds necessary for the role of practitioner-researcher. Learners are being invited to question the practice, to reflect on it, and to solve questions about it. Here, then, is the changing ethos in teaching: students are expected to discover things for themselves, and discovery learning is the beginning of research. It is in continuing education, however, that this approach has found a significant place.

Continuing Education of Practitioner-Researchers

The preparation of practitioner-researchers has emerged to a tremendous extent through the development of continuing professional education. Continuing education has changed the face of universities. Once the main student group was the eighteen- to twenty-five-year-olds, but now things have changed. Campbell (1984) points out that by 1974–75, adult learners in credit and noncredit courses in Canada had become the majority among university students. This has no doubt been true ever since for most universities in North America and in the United Kingdom as well. Lifelong education has become generally accepted, and most universities now cater to older students as well as to young adults. Master's degrees and practitioner doctorates are now the main product of many university departments. Professionals who come to the university on day or block release (that is, released by their employer to spend a period away from work to study) are among the new breed of practitioner-researchers. The development of the M.B.A. has meant that management recognizes the need to develop more research, and managers themselves are researching their practice.

Indeed, some graduate programs positively encourage the practitioner-researcher. In the school of education in which I teach, we run a number of master's degree programs and a taught doctorate (as opposed to a research-only doctorate), and among the entry qualifications are two important ones: the candidates for the course are normally expected to be in practice and to have had two years' practical experience before we will admit them. This is true of the adult education course, the program in change agent skills, and the newly launched program in management consultancy. Note that some of these courses are run face to face, but others are conducted at a distance—we have students in more than thirty countries, all of whom are being encouraged to use their own practice for their assignments.

Students are asked to work in peer learning groups using e-mail and other means of contact when the course is run at a distance, to write up critical moments from their own practice in a learning log, and to use their practice as the basis of investigations for coursework activities and assignments. All the assignments are about their own practical knowledge as they reflect on it and research their practice. An introductory assignment to one of the modules on theories of teaching, for instance, merely asks the students to send the assessor a copy of a lesson plan they have taught recently and to justify the content and process described therein. Apparently simple, this opening assignment makes the ordinary everyday lesson the focus of a great deal of reflection and perhaps some research. Suddenly, the teacher is no longer just a teacher but a reflective practitioner or practitioner-researcher. In other assignments, the candidates are asked to produce research reports on incidents in their practice or otherwise to focus on firsthand job experiences.

In some of the programs, we actually specify that we expect the participants not to apply the theory we give them to their practice but rather to try it out and see if it works for them. If it does, they should accept it and try to figure out why it is useful; if it does not, they should reject it, after determining why it was unsuccessful. In a sense, we are asking them to produce their own theory and practice, relevant to them in their particular situation. This is not their "theory in use" (Argyris and Schön, [1974] 1992), which conveys the idea of something quite static, but rather their evolving theory and their own body of current knowledge as they continue to develop their own practice.

All of these programs finish with a research project in which the students frequently use their own practice as the basis of their research. They produce research dissertations of high quality—some of them have been published. Courses of this nature, grounded in the students' practice, turn out practitioner-researchers.

Underlying the philosophy of all of these programs is the recognition that individuals learn during the daily processes of working and living. This learning is most frequently incidental (Marsick and Watkins, 1990). But the term *incidental learning* conveys the wrong idea—it seems to imply *accidental* learning. Yet throughout human history, most learning has been incidental: when we confront a problem, we seek to solve it and act to apply our solution. Thus, that we have actually learned may not always be recognized if the prime objective is to solve a practical problem. Revans (1982) called this *action learning*; the term captures the idea that learning should result in action, and much of it in today's world is in the workplace.

In a similar way, doctoral students have also been encouraged to research their own practice. An example of this was a research project on the role of the human resource development (HRD) officer in an organization. The research entailed keeping a diary on the role for eighteen months, recording all the interactions with all members of staff, all the activities undertaken, and so on. This diary became part of the data analyzed for the doctorate, and the final outcome of the project is a handbook for HRD specialists (Hargreaves and Jarvis, 1998).

In the same way as I have recorded this research project from one of my own doctoral students, I could have reported on doctoral research that I have read recently from South Africa and Australia—for instance, a project by an educator working as a consultant with a large automobile manufacturer in South Africa revealed how the vocational learning the workers were undertaking was also changing their perspectives about other aspects of their lives in that country. The doctoral candidate researched the wider effects of his own practice.

The introduction of continuing professional development has had other unexpected consequences. Eurich (1985) reports on Digital Equipment's corporation manager for educational services, Del Lippert, who speaks "with conviction and detailed knowledge of the company's research on the ways people approach learning. Their analysis—more directly cognitive than Kolb's for experiential learning—leads to combinations of four approaches: concrete, abstract, sequential, and random" (p. 57). As large corporations introduce their own professional development, they find themselves becoming researchers in order to undertake their training more effectively. Now we have the corporate university—which is not merely a teaching and training institution. These new institutions are introducing research-based projects into their own practice.

Continuing professional education has thus provided a major impetus in the development of practitioner-researchers. Indeed, the conditions are right and the growth will no doubt continue unabated.

Conclusion

In this chapter we have looked at what is probably the major way in which practitioner-researchers are stimulated and trained. On the day when I was writing this, however, an incident occurred that demonstrated quite clearly that management itself is also stimulating practitioner research. A colleague who is a manager told me that she could not make an important management decision we were discussing without sufficient information, so she had asked a practitioner to provide her with precise data about the course she was organizing. The course organizer therefore had to go and seek more information about her own practice—she became a practitioner-researcher. This is not unusual; it happens all the time—and that is just the point. Practitioners are being asked to research their practice continually.

Ironically, this basis of decision making is technical-rational in form—the very approach to rationality that Schön (1983) attacked so comprehensively. Nevertheless, it still seems to make common sense to us, and a great deal of management theory is grounded in this rather false technical-rational approach to practice.

Education, training, and management are almost inadvertently creating practitioner-researchers. Such people are emerging all the time, but they are still rarely recognized for what they are. Now we have to ask, why does practice demand all this research? That is the focus of the following chapter.

Chapter Three

Researching Practice

For a number of years now, the modern approaches to professional preparation have meant that it is no longer surprising to hear the site of practice referred to as a place of reflective learning. Since Schön (1983), *reflective practitioner* has rightly become a commonplace term. But it is also becoming increasingly common to find practitioners researching their practice, as we have seen in the first two chapters. Can practitioner-researchers really research their own practice? Why do practitioners do such research? These are the first questions that this chapter addresses. Thereafter I examine the nature of practice itself.

Can Practitioner-Researchers Research Their Own Practice?

Traditionally, the scientific researcher endeavored to remain objective and to measure or record data in as detached a manner as possible. It might be asked, therefore, how can practitioner-researchers fulfill this basic criterion of research when they are actually involved in researching, often researching their own practice? To respond to this question, let us examine the following episode.

Titchen (1996) records a situation in a collaborative research project with a nurse. The expert nurse decided that it was not right to wash a patient who was in severe pain at that moment but that it would be better to await the effects of an analgesic first. The patient's daughter, however, arrived before the nurse was able to wash the patient and immediately implicitly criticized the nurse for not having washed her parent. Yet the nurse's decision not to act was a positive act. She had made a decision that was right for her, but an observer wrongly interpreted the decision not to act. The expert nurse recorded how she read the situation and decided how she could involve the patient's daughter in helping to wash her parent and so overcome both an implicit criticism of her performance and a potentially difficult interview explaining her actions to the daughter without appearing on the defensive.

Only the expert nurse herself, or as in this case, the nurse as a co-researcher in a collaborative research project, could have recorded all the nuances of this scene. Traditional scientific research would almost certainly have failed to catch the flavor of the situation, the decision not to act, the reflection-in-action of the nurse at the arrival of the patient's daughter, and other nuances. Indeed, this situation might have been unusual for the expert nurse and therefore might not have been captured in a sample survey. It is certainly a situation that is not easily replicable. Only through qualitative and in-depth involvement in the practice could the richness of this potentially problematic situation have been recorded. Practitioner-researchers are able to report aspects of practice at a depth that traditional forms of research might well not capture, precisely because they are practitioners. Their research can be enriched if it is undertaken in collaboration.

Why Do Practitioners Research Their Own Practice?

Practitioners research their own practice for a number of reasons, including that we live in a knowledge society that is always changing, that experts advise the powerful, and that continuing education is a way of gaining qualifications that will assist the career advancement of practitioners. I deal here with each of these reasons in turn.

Knowledge Society

Advanced capitalist societies such as the United States are technological societies. Ever since the Reformation of the sixteenth century,
the importance of science and scientific knowledge has been growing. This was emphasized by the Enlightenment thinkers of the eighteenth century and has consequently become a central tenet of
modernity. Many occupations have, to a very great extent, become
knowledge-based. Reich (1991) calls the knowledge workers *symbolic
analysts*; other scholars use the term *knowledge-based workers* (Stehr,
1994). The significant thing about scientific knowledge, however, is
that it has always been research-based. As a result, knowledge-based
occupations, such as nursing, have more recently referred to themselves as research-based and evidence-based professions.

The reason for this equation is easy to see, since these occupations have endeavored to professionalize and produce their own bodies of knowledge. Indeed, a senior management consultant told me
quite forcefully that it was essential that the management consultancy industry produced its own body of knowledge so that it could
gain the status of a profession. Professionals have always been regarded as experts, and in the knowledge-based society, experts are
regarded as experts only when they have the most up-to-date knowledge uncovered by scientific research. But scientific knowledge
changes rapidly, as Scheler pointed out as early as 1926. Indeed,
Scheler claimed that scientific knowledge changed "hour by hour"
(Stikkers, 1980, p. 76). No doubt he would now be saying that it
changes by the second in contemporary society.

It is this rapid social change that makes contemporary society
reflexive (Beck, 1992). Giddens (1990) summarizes this position
nicely: "The reflexivity of modern social life consists in the fact that
social practices are constantly examined and reformed in the light of
incoming information about those very practices, thus constitutively
altering their character. . . . All forms of social life are partly constituted by actors' knowledge of them. Knowing 'how to go on' . . .

is intrinsic to the conventions which are drawn upon and repro-
duced by human activity. In all cultures, social practices are routinely
altered in the light of on-going discoveries which feed upon them"
(p. 38).

Basically, Giddens is saying that everything is changing all the
time, partly driven by the state of knowledge at the time, and as
more information is discovered the practice changes in response to
it, in an ongoing cycle. The more we know, the more we introduce
change, and the more we need to reflect on it. We need to discover
if we have the best solution, since we have found out that the
knowledge we have about the practices we undertake is not necessarily to be equated with the certainty that we have the best solution—so the more we need to research. Research, then, is built into
the very nature of the type of society in which we live, and all aspir-
ing experts must have researched and discovered the most recent
knowledge about their practice in order to be experts.

Experts Advising Managers

Chapter Two ended with the illustration of a colleague in a managerial role generating research about practice from a junior colleague merely by asking for information to be used in decision
making. Experts have always advised the power holders. Managers
are not always experts in the areas they manage, so they make decisions based on the advice of others.

In this managerial society, more managers are being trained to
make technical-rational decisions based on expert advice, and
more practitioners are being asked to research the information necessary for the managers to make those decisions. But those decisions are not necessarily correct, because technical rationality is not
necessarily the most beneficial way to make all decisions. This paradox has led to what Beck (1992) calls the *risk society*. But it is an
almost inevitable outcome of the type of society that has emerged
from the Enlightenment.

Career

In the knowledge society, it is essential that professional practitioners become specialists and experts; consequently, undertaking continuing professional education is necessary to keep abreast, to be seen as keeping abreast, and to gain qualifications that might lead to career advancement. Therefore, more practitioners are studying for higher degrees, and more practitioner-researchers are being generated.

There are, however, motives beyond career advancement for practitioner research. In the past few years, a number of my doctoral students have reached the end of their professional careers and have enrolled and paid their own fees to undertake research. A nurse educator and a radiologist educator both undertook research at the end of their careers so they could put something back into their professions. The nurse educator told me she felt that she had gained a lot from her profession and owed it a great deal; by undertaking this research and publishing her findings, she could repay some of her debt. Both of these people gained research degrees, and national honors, at about the same time as they retired from their senior positions in their respective professions.

Similarly, an amateur sports coach wanted to learn more about coaches and coaching, so when he retired from his full-time job, he sponsored himself to do research for a Ph.D. He continues his coaching, but now he is a practitioner-researcher among sports coaches. Perhaps we are beginning to see yet another type of researcher-practitioner: individuals who undertake research as intellectual stimulation in their leisure time.

Discovering knowledge is a direct consequence of the forces that led to this world of modernity. Nevertheless, the type of research undertaken and much of the knowledge discovered by practitioner-researchers might be an indication that we are moving into a new era, because neither the research nor the type of knowledge generated would necessarily fulfill the criteria of "pure" science. Significantly, modernity is not over, but the new approaches to research indicate that many of the values of modernity are open to question. We are moving into a new era—late modernity—but it is not replacing modernity; it is merely a new phase, one of reflexive modernity (Giddens, 1990; Beck, 1992). The emergence of practitioner-researchers is itself a symbol of this reflexivity.

Having discussed the idea of researching practice, we now need to understand something more about the nature of practice itself. The remainder of this chapter highlights some important features about it.

The Nature of Practice

It is now commonplace to write about the speed of change and the management of change (Sadler, 1995). Everything is changing at a rapid rate, and the causes are multitudinous. Among these are the processes of automation and globalization, the introduction of advanced information technology, and new scientific research. Occasionally, internal innovations also result in changes that create more efficient production lines, and so on. All of these changes call for new knowledge and new techniques and skills among practitioners. The fluidity of the environment has affected the way people work and live. Reich (1991), for instance, suggests that about one-third of all workers will be "symbolic analysts"—people who work with this rapidly changing knowledge—and the remainder will have to adapt their work lives to fit into this new world. The plethora of new forms of knowledge, new skills, and new techniques, however, that have been introduced means that everybody's field of practice is affected in different ways.

A field of practice is an area of operation or activity, a site at which an occupation is performed. It is not a geographical location so much as a territory. The field of practice of university teaching, for instance, has been the university, and the field of practice for nursing has been the hospital ward. In a similar manner, the field of practice for a bird watcher has usually been the countryside, although in more recent times it has also become urban locations.

The fact that it has become an urban activity as well points to the fact that fields of practice are changing, often rapidly. The field of practice of an adult educator, for instance, is much more difficult to determine—it might be the university or the workplace or the community college or the community itself, or a combination of any of these locales.

It is possible to see fields of professional practice in terms of both internal structures and external boundaries, and the changes are having their effects on both and are spilling over into adjacent occupations. Fields are often being completely redefined. As noted earlier, Giroux (1992) questions the external structures of school education and seeks "to broaden the parameters of how we think about schooling, pedagogy and cultural politics" (p. 2). Eurich (1985) has also recorded how the corporate classroom is having its effect on the structures of higher education in the United States. Thus we see that the boundaries between higher education and the world of work are themselves being redefined. Similarly, we are seeing the boundaries between adult and higher education disappear as more adults return to university to continue their professional education.

In precisely the same manner, the internal structures of teaching adults are open to question: should teachers of adults be trained to teach in the classroom, or should they be trained as human resource developers, mentors, counselors, administrators, assessors, program planners, authors of learning materials, and so on (Jarvis, 1995)? This list reflects some of the ways in which my own work has changed since I entered university teaching. When I began, I never considered that I might be writing distance-learning units for a program that would have students in nearly three dozen countries, or that the units would appear on the World Wide Web, or that I would be trying to establish centers to host our program in different parts of the world, or that I would be negotiating with private organizations to enter into partnerships with the university. All of these things have occurred in the past few years; the world of practice has changed drastically, and consequently I have to keep acquiring new skills and new knowledge.

In a similar way, major shifts in health care have generated debates about the extent to which more technology should be introduced and the extent to which providers of health care need to adjust their practices to incorporate these changes. The use of high-technology procedures has also raised a great number of new ethical problems for practitioners. In addition, we are seeing different specialisms converge and new ones emerge as strategies for health care change in the light of social and economic forces.

Management consultancy has come to recognize that the role of consultants has changed from being involved in strategy and process to being change agents and human resource specialists and even undertaking management tasks in the organization for the period of the contract to operationalize their own recommendations. Such changes are occurring in almost all occupations; as a result, both continuing education and work-based learning have become features of work itself.

The fact that practice is a locus of change means that learning and researching practice are essential for practitioners in novel situations; they may not have sufficient knowledge to act with complete confidence in such situations, and no theory exists about these new situations—practice must precede theory in such instances if the theory is to appertain directly to the practice.

Practice is always changing. Individual practitioners are learning and researching how to respond in their changing situations, so a number of conclusions can be drawn about the nature of practice from the discussion in this chapter:

- Practice is transitory rather than empirical and unchanging.
- Knowledge about practice cannot be measured.
- Practice is a personal and subjective phenomenon to the practitioner.
- Precise events can never be repeated, so each practice situation is unique.
- To understand practice fully, it is necessary to undertake qualitative research.

- Any research undertaken about practice can only be a snap-shot of the events that occur when the research takes place.
- Any published data from research must be treated from a historical perspective, as something relevant to the time when the research was undertaken.

You might ask, then, whether there is any place for quantitative research in seeking to understand practice. Naturally, there are many things about practice that demand quantitative answers—education managers must know the number of staff, the number of students, the cost of running a school, and so on. This would be true for any manager, whatever the organization or occupation. Managers need quantitative data on which to make decisions. In addition, empirical, longitudinal studies may also reveal trends in the way that the field of practice is changing. Many of these types of survey are reported in practitioner journals.

Practitioner-researchers might be involved in small surveys gathering quantitative data, especially when they are asked to provide information for managerial decisions—but then any researcher can gather such data. What is special about the practitioner-researchers' role is that they can record the more personal, subjective aspects of this ephemeral phenomenon of practice.

Conclusion

Practitioner-researchers are both practitioners and researchers and, for heuristic purposes only, the two roles are split in the next two parts of this book. In Part Two I look at some of the areas of practice that the large-scale research project might miss, and in Part Three I look at the research processes that practitioner-researchers can employ to discover those data.

Part Two

The Nature of Practice

Chapter Four

The Practitioner's Knowledge

I know a minister of religion who talks of his professional training. He had an excellent theological preparation: he studied Hebrew, Greek, and Latin (languages of the Bible and the early church), church history, theology, the Bible, and so on. He gained a good university degree in theology. But the first time he ever considered conducting a wedding or a funeral was when he became the minister of a parish church and had to perform one. He actually had had no practical preparation at all. He knew a lot about the theology of the denomination of which he had become a minister, but nothing at all about actually being a minister.

In short, he had mastered the high-status subjects that classified his occupation as a profession. He had learned his theory—"knowledge why," in the terms used previously—but he had not learned any "knowledge how."

In this chapter we are going to consider how practitioners learn their practical knowledge, and we shall do so in four areas: the nature of theory, the nature of knowledge, practical knowledge, and tacit knowledge.

The Nature of Theory

In the example, we can see that at the time about which the minister was speaking, having a knowledge of theology was regarded as more important to the church in which he was trained than any other form of preparation. It was regarded as the church's theory, and learning it preceded practice.

I have already noted the significance of the body of researched knowledge, or theory, for occupations that are professionalizing. It is essential for them that there be a body of knowledge underlying the profession. Yet that body of knowledge is drawn together in a formal manner in only two separate situations:

- When an occupation formally constructs its body of knowledge—the management consultancy industry in the United Kingdom, for instance, has published its body of knowledge on the World Wide Web.
- When a professional school or college develops its curriculum for preparing new entrants to the profession. Frequently, professional associations seek to validate or in some other way legitimate these curricula, often by providing membership in the relevant professional association upon successful completion of the program.

Significantly, the content of the two need not be the same, although they ought to have some resemblance to each other.

There are four main sources from which these curricula, or bodies of knowledge, are developed:

- Research reports and articles published in journals
- Books about the occupation
- Input from experienced practitioners, who may or may not be practicing (they may now be professors, managers, or administrators for professional associations, for example)
- Relevant knowledge from other disciplines and practices

Almost the first thing we notice about this list is that all of these sources are from the past, albeit the recent past, but they are still historical. Books and papers report work that has been conducted in the past, the experienced professionals are recalling their own past experiences, and the relevant knowledge from other disciplines is also usually drawn from previous research. The theory taught in professional schools reflects a past rather than a current situation, but the new entrants to the profession are being prepared for a future one.

Yet one of the points that became very clear in Chapter Three was that things are changing rapidly and that practice itself is transitory, almost ephemeral. We are therefore confronted with the problem of the relationship between theory and practice that was raised in Chapter Three. Seeking to overcome that problem has been one of the reasons why there have been so many innovations in professional preparation, as we saw in Chapter Two.

What, then, do these professional curricula contain? It would require a research project to examine the curricula in different professions to compare them; this would certainly make a very interesting comparative exercise. We can use, however, an example from teacher training, reflecting my own experience in the preparation of schoolteachers and adult educators. Students are taught

- The history of education
- Some relevant practices, such as teaching, learning, program planning, assessing, and evaluating
- Some of the academic disciplines that have studied education, such as philosophy and sociology

In addition, they have a number of school visits and internships, although the minister of religion referred to at the start of this chapter certainly had no internship in his preparation.

If we look at this curriculum, we see that the students are given the opportunity to learn some process knowledge (knowledge how) and some content knowledge (knowledge why). This is the theory they taught, and it is often treated as if it is universally true and that is why they have to learn it. The students also have some opportunities to learn to be able to do. The knowledge how and the knowledge why, taken together, are what I want to call "mediated knowledge" gained through secondary experiences, whereas the learning to be able to do is learning from primary (firsthand) experience.

To lay the foundation for the discussion, I refer briefly to my own research on learning (Jarvis, 1987, 1992), although there are many other works on learning to which I could have also referred (for example, Kolb, 1984; Boud, Keogh, and Walker, 1985; Brookfield, 1986; Merriam and Caffarella, 1991). From my own research, I formulated the model of learning depicted in Figure 4.1. I do not want to develop all the aspects of this model here, although it is important to examine boxes 1 through 3 now. These boxes show a process: a person enters a situation and creates a subjective experience. That situation can be a lecture hall or classroom or the workplace. In the academic setting, I have a primary experience of sitting in the classroom, and a mediated secondary experience, which is the theory that I am taught and, ideally, learn. In the workplace, I have a primary experience of the physical space and the actual work about which I might be taught but from which I also learn.

Now, there are four routes from the experience:

- To box 4—the route I take if I do not learn (nonlearning)
- To box 6—the route I take if I merely memorize (nonreflective learning)
- To box 7—the route I take if I reflect on my experience and then learn (reflective learning)
- To box 5—the route I take if I practice what I have learned (learning by doing, nonreflective and/or reflective)

I do not learn from my experience if I can presume upon it and act in a taken-for-granted manner. But if there is disjuncture between my biography (the sum of my experiences, both conscious and unconscious) and a particular experience, I might seek to learn to close it. For instance, when I am introduced to a stranger at a party, I will put out my hand to shake hands—I will do this automatically and unthinkingly. Naturally I expect the stranger to whom I am being introduced to do the same, but if he does not, I have to think quickly about how I am to behave. My learning begins from this situation; in a sense, all learning begins with an ex-

Figure 4.1. A Model of the Learning Processes.

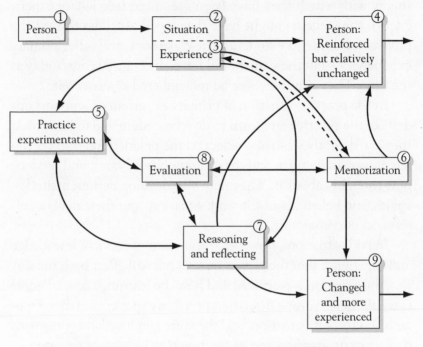

Source: Jarvis, 1992, p. 71. Used by permission of Jossey-Bass, Publishers.

perience of disjuncture—what Mezirow (Mezirow and Associates, 1990, p. 14) calls a "disorienting dilemma"—whether it is induced by others or by myself.

Naturally, all of these responses to experience, except the first, then progress through different routes to learning, since there are different types of learning going on. In addition, these learning processes can, and do, occur simultaneously, so I can do, reflect, and memorize at the same time. What I have described here oversimplifies the argument I have presented elsewhere, but it is sufficient for this discussion, so we can now return to our students.

When the students have mediated secondary experiences— that is, when they are taught theory—they can either memorize or reflect on it and then memorize the outcomes of their deliberations. In the process of learning, the students have also taken someone else's knowledge and made it their own. In addition to learning the theory with which they have been presented (secondary experiences), the students might have developed attitudes toward the professor, their fellow students, the classroom, and other primary experiences—but these might not have all occurred consciously at the time. They may, however, be remembered at a later date.

In the practice situation of primary experiences, students undertake the practice and learn to do a procedure and to know that they can do it; they can also reflect on the practice and think of different ways of doing it, and they can theorize about it and produce new thoughts about it. They may also develop certain attitudes, values, and beliefs about the work situation, and these may not always occur consciously.

In both situations, however, the amount of previous knowledge and experience that the person (box 1) has will affect both the way that the situation is perceived and how the learning occurs. People carry all their learning from their previous experiences (their biography) into every situation, and these are employed in coping with their current situation and in creating new individual experiences for themselves from which they learn.

Learning is therefore the process of creating and transforming experience into knowledge, skills, attitudes, values, emotions, senses, and beliefs.

But how do the students know that what they are learning in professional school is true? They can either accept its validity because they accept the authority of the professor who has taught them—so they memorize it in a nonreflective manner—or they can reflect on it and reach conclusions about it based on their own logical reasoning. What they have learned, therefore, has become their own knowledge, but they have accepted its validity for different reasons. Perhaps the professor had got the facts wrong, so the students' confidence was misplaced and the knowledge they learned was incorrect. We would claim, therefore, that it is better that the students think about things critically for themselves before they accept what they are taught as true (Brookfield, 1987; Meyers, 1986). But we know that this is not always the case. Nevertheless, there is a sense in which the theory taught in professional school or university is generally regarded as true and treated as if it were knowledge, rather than information or belief that has not yet been proved— even if it was true only in the past.

But this argument does not apply to students learning during internship. Student teachers are not relying on the authority of their professors to make sure that they have a successful lesson, nor does critical thinking about the knowledge that they learned in the college of education necessarily mean than they can teach a class. They have to try out their knowledge in the practice situation before they can trust it. To understand the relationship between these various ways of knowing, it might now be useful to look briefly at the nature of knowledge itself.

The Nature of Knowledge

The *Concise Oxford Dictionary* (1996) defines *knowledge* in the following ways: "awareness or familiarity gained by experience"; "a person's range of information"; "a theoretical or a practical understanding of a subject"; "the sum of what is known"; "something which is true as opposed to a belief or an opinion." In contrast to these definitions, a dictionary of philosophy (Flew, 1979) offers the following distinctions: "knowledge that—factual knowledge"; "knowledge how—practical knowledge"; and "knowledge of— knowledge of people and places." We can immediately recognize that these different definitions of knowledge reflect our foregoing discussion. What makes these different types of knowledge true?

Knowledge can be legitimated in at least three different ways: rationalistically, empirically, and pragmatically (Scheffler, 1965).

The *rationalist* form of knowledge comes from the exercise of reason. Pure mathematics is often the example provided for knowledge of this type; mathematicians need no objects beyond the problem and no form of proof that is not to be found within its own logic, so its conclusions rest entirely on its own argument. Philosophical knowledge might also be regarded as another form of knowledge that is legitimated in the same way. This form of knowledge is legitimated by the process of reason.

Empirical knowledge relies on sensory experiences; knowledge is true if it can be shown to relate to a tangible phenomenon. Thus I know that there is something on which I am sitting—I can feel it and I do not sink to the ground when I sit down. I know through my senses that there is an object here; even though the concept of "chair" is not a sensory experience, the object is. We can have knowledge of a reality beyond ourselves through our senses.

The *pragmatist* emphasizes the experimental nature of certain forms of experience: I try something out and find that it either works or fails, whatever the case may be. I learn that the chair I am sitting on will support me, and until such time as it lets me down I will continue to assume that fact. Change the situation, and I might need to change the performance for it to be successful, thereby perhaps changing the associated knowledge. This is a very practical form of knowledge. It implies that there is nothing other than the practice itself—there may not be a generalizable truth or an empirical reality underlying it.

If we now return to the nature of theory, we can see that the knowledge that is included in the body of knowledge or the curriculum might have been legitimated by any one of the three modes. But that legitimation happened in the past, and when the students learn it, they accept it either because they accept the authority of the professor or because they have applied their own reasoning and legitimated it for themselves rationally.

By contrast, the knowledge they learn in practice, even in an internship, is entirely pragmatic. This is also true when they are in practice itself. Pragmatism works! But an apparent problem with it is that everything appears to be relative and there are no universal values or generalizable truths underlying the experimental data. If I try out the art of stealing and find that I am successful, I can begin to develop my own knowledge about being a successful thief. But I can also use precisely the same argument about being a successful minister of religion, doctor, nurse, or teacher.

Consider the following example. A salesperson sells to clients life insurance policies that have poor returns, but the policies seem cheap, the salesperson is convincing, and his clients are not experts in financial matters. He is regarded as successful because his technique obviously works. Another salesperson is more concerned that her clients get a good return on their investment, even though the policies are a little more expensive initially. She does not get as many sales, and her techniques are not regarded as so effective. The salesman might be regarded as the better salesperson by his company because he gets more sales. The saleswoman, however, might actually be more honest and get a better deal for her clients. To overcome some of these ethical problems, many professions seek to publish their codes of ethics, and a few companies are beginning to publish customer charters.

Pragmatism is about discovering what works for each of us; it is not about generalizations. Even so, what is successful for one of us might also be useful in helping others develop their own practices, as the practice of pairing practitioners in the work situation has demonstrated (Yakowicz, 1987). We have to be careful, however, not to assume that because something works for one or even a few persons it is necessarily going to work for every practitioner of the same occupation in every situation. We cannot generalize in this manner, but we can see that learning from experience is individuating and, perhaps, fragmenting.

What is clear, however, is that the pragmatic seems to be assuming a dominance in advanced capitalist and technological societies because it reflects the nature and needs of these societies. Lyotard (1984), the French social philosopher, suggested that all knowledge is narrative increasingly legitimated by performability, although he later modified his assertion and claimed that much knowledge is narrative (Lyotard, 1992). He has not, however, modified his views about pragmatism. Indeed, the type of knowledge that we learn in practice is pragmatic.

This is the form of knowledge with which we are all familiar. Heller (1984) points out that our "everyday thinking and everyday behaviour are primarily pragmatic." She goes on, interestingly enough, to suggest that the "pragmatic relationship denotes the direct unity of theory and practice" (p. 166). Chisholm (1988) also regards a person's intentional attitudes as the point at which theory and practice meet.

Nevertheless, there are many similarities in the way people behave both in everyday life and in professional practice. This is because we share the same language, similar practice sites, and the understanding of practice gained through the normal processes of observation and conversation. We can learn from others *about* practice, but ultimately we must learn *how to* practice by doing it. This is also true for other practitioners. The only way to learn to tango is to tango. It is hardly surprising that a degree of similarity emerges in what is learned and practiced, but we accept it only if it works for us.

This similarity does not constitute objective knowledge—knowledge "out there," as it were; it is intersubjective. We share similar situations and learn similar things. Though our similarities appear to constitute objective knowledge, they are actually no more than objectifications. Indeed, they are also information rather than knowledge. Objectification is precisely the process that has been undertaken in the construction of theory.

Consequently, we can make a distinction between theory, which is information to be learned by students according to the rational processes, if it is to become their knowledge; and that which is learned by practitioners according to the pragmatic processes, if it is to become their practical knowledge.

Practical Knowledge

In my everyday life, I use practical knowledge all the time. For instance, when I go into a shop and attempt to get the attention of a sales clerk, I am using my everyday knowledge. I interact with the clerk on the assumption that we speak the same language, that he has the same understanding of the norms of everyday behavior as other people with whom I have interacted, and so forth. If I want to get the best service from him, I will naturally be courteous and thoughtful, and when the transaction is completed, I will depart amicably. But I did not consciously think that to get the best service I should use a little bit of applied psychology, a little social theory, and so on, or that I should take these techniques from their respective disciplines and apply them to practice.

I might have considered how best to attract the clerk's attention in a busy shop; I may have recognized that if I was too demanding, for instance, I might not get the most efficient service and that I should wait until he had finished talking to another customer before I tried to attract his attention. What I am using in these instances is practical knowledge, which can, for the purposes of understanding, be broken down into knowledge how, knowledge when, knowledge what, knowledge that, and knowledge why but in practice are fused together as practical knowledge. Significantly, they are never subdivided into academic disciplines.

When I visit my medical doctor, however, she uses the same type of process knowledge in the interaction—but she also uses her specialist medical knowledge in her diagnosis. When she prescribes treatment for me, it might be because she has used similar treatment for other people with my condition and she knows that it works (pragmatic) or because she has read about the treatment in a medical journal and thinks that it will work in my case (rational knowledge). If it does, she will incorporate it into her general usage because she has proved it pragmatically for herself. By contrast, she will reject it if she discovers that it might have worked under controlled laboratory conditions but was unsuccessful in real life.

Practical knowledge, be it process or content knowledge, is therefore always pragmatic for the practitioner. Process knowledge, however, is totally integrated and will never have been subdivided by the practitioners into the various academic disciplines.

In practice, then, I build up my own body of knowledge about my practice by learning, doing, thinking, and reflecting on what I do. It is my body of knowledge about my own practice. It began with the theory I learned in the classroom (including the knowledge I learned

from the disciplines relevant to my practice), continued as I practiced and watched others in the practice situation from which I also
learned, and developed even further as I practiced and thought about
and reflected on what I had done. For as long as I continue in practice, the process will continue. The moment I leave practice, however, for whatever reason—including to teach it—I cease to learn
from it and begin to learn about it, and my expertise gradually dete-
riorates. Consequently, most teachers of practical occupations endeavor to continue in practice, even if only on a part-time basis, in
order to retain their expertise.

We are now in a position to summarize about the practitioners'
own knowledge:

- Practical knowledge is the practitioner's own knowledge that
  has been legitimated in practice. It is personal and qualitative. Its legitimation is that it works for me, and because it
  does, I develop my own ways of doing things in accordance
  with my own values, beliefs, and feelings. There is a sense,
  therefore, that as my actions are legitimated by their own
  success, this leads to an inevitability that I will repeat my
  actions. This is a process of habituation, which in turn generates a certain form of traditionalism. This has led to practitioners being regarded as conservative by researchers and
  theorists. But the question practitioners legitimately ask is,
  why change if what I do works for me and I am happy with it?
  There may well be major reasons that change is necessary, but
  practitioners need to be convinced of this, and then it may be
  not only their practice that will need to be changed but also
  their situation.

- Practical knowledge is a combination of process knowledge and
  content knowledge, which includes relevant knowledge of the
  academic disciplines that underlies practice.

- Practical knowledge is practical, not merely the application of
  some "pure" academic discipline to practical situations.

- Practical knowledge is integrated knowledge.

- Practical knowledge is dynamic only as long as it works.
- Practical knowledge is not an academic discipline in the same way as the sciences or the social sciences. For instance, I can have a body of knowledge about education, which can be taught, and I can have a sociology of education, but I cannot have an education of sociology or a nursing of philosophy. Hence it is necessary to draw a distinction between the field of practice, about which I develop my own practical knowledge, and academic disciplines (again a problematic concept to which we shall return), like sociology, psychology and economics.

The complexity of the situations in which I practice and the experiences from which I learn mean that as I become more expert in my practice I might concentrate on some dimensions of my experience rather than on others. I might not, therefore, always retain all my knowledge in my conscious mind, so that I appear to act almost intuitively. This is the tacit dimension.

Tacit Knowledge

Many experienced practitioners have the feeling that "we can know more than we can tell" (Polanyi, 1967, p. 4), which is this tacit dimension. Polanyi points out that we can pick out a face from among a million different ones, but we cannot necessarily describe the person accurately. He recognized that when we focus on specific elements in an experience, we usually see others less consciously but can still give meaning to the whole. This is the tacit dimension to our experience.

In a similar manner, when we habituate our actions, we might be aware of precisely what we are doing, but we often find it difficult, if not impossible, to specify it. Nyiri (1988, pp. 20–21) writes, quoting Feigenbaum and McCorduck (1984):

> One becomes an expert not simply by absorbing explicit knowledge of the type found in textbooks, but through experience, that is,

through repeated trials, "failing, succeeding, wasting time and effort, getting a feel for a problem, learning when to go by the book and when to break the rules." Human experts thereby gradually absorb "a repertoire of working rules of thumb, or 'heuristics,' that, combined with book knowledge, make them expert practitioners." This practical, heuristic knowledge, as attempts to simulate it on the machine have shown, is "hardest to get at because experts—or anyone else—rarely have the self-awareness to recognize what it is. So it must be mined out of their heads painstakingly, one jewel at a time.

Picardi (1988) defines tacit knowledge in a similar manner, as the "type of knowledge which, even though it can somehow be manifested, need not, and in many cases cannot be articulated *linguistically*" (p. 91, italics in original). Not all knowledge is narrative or discourse.

Tacit knowledge, then, is learned from experience, either preconsciously—that is, without having entered the conscious mind—or consciously, and has been forgotten or even repressed. Most important, we can presume tacitly precisely because doing so does work for us. The very essence of tacitness is pragmatic. When we enter different situations, we are able to call on reserves of taken-for-granted knowledge that we cannot articulate. Because it works, we can continue to presume on it. Consequently, we do not learn from it—or else we learn in a preconscious manner. Unlike Nyiri, I want to suggest that tacit knowledge not only is the knowledge of experts but also is present in all forms of practical knowledge.

Schön (1983, p. 54) makes similar points about professionals' practical knowledge. He suggests that professionals know how to carry out actions spontaneously, are not always aware of having learned to do these things, and are usually unable to describe the knowing that the action needs. Tacit knowledge, then, can occur in knowledge how, when, that, what, and why. Since all learning is biographical, this tacit dimension is also built into our own biographies, and we all act in a taken-for-granted manner without necessarily being able to articulate the how or the why.

Figure 4.2. The Nature of Practical Knowledge.

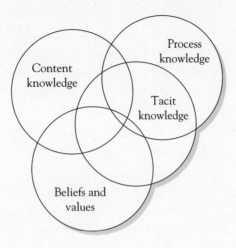

We are now in a position to depict the knowledge of practition-ers as shown in Figure 4.2. Practical knowledge is a sophisticated and uniquely subjective combination of the types of knowledge that work for us.

Conclusion

Through learning from practical experience, practitioners take the content of what they are taught and what they acquire in practice, and they build their own theory. This theory is pragmatic, neces-sarily dynamic, and relative to the practice situation—to which we turn our attention in Chapter Five.

Chapter Five

Practicing

By definition, all practitioner-researchers are practitioners, and as we have already suggested, they will almost certainly research their practice, so the aim of this chapter is to examine how practitioners perform their roles in an ever-changing practice situation. Even if it were not changing, the actual act of practice would change all the time, since practitioners are not machines undertaking precisely the same procedure in exactly the same manner each time. Human behavior may be patterned, but it is rarely machinelike.

For the sake of clarity I have separated this discussion about practicing from the discussion of how practitioners learn their own theory, although I must acknowledge that the two processes occur simultaneously. I demonstrate this in Chapter Six, on reflective practice. The discussion in this chapter is subdivided into four sections: becoming an expert, habituating, the *habitus*, and doing and being.

Becoming an Expert

Newcomers to an occupation enter practice with the theory they have learned from secondary experience and legitimated by their own rational thinking or by the authority they have ascribed to their professors. But in practice, they have to make that theory their own, to legitimate it by their own pragmatic practice. In the process, they not only learn the practical knowledge but also acquire appropriate skills.

Lave and Wenger (1991) suggest that the newcomers are required to move toward full participation in the sociocultural practices of the community: "Legitimate peripheral participation provides a way to speak about the relations between newcomers and old-timers, about activities, identities, artefacts, and communities of knowledge and practice" (p. 29). Many years earlier, Goffman (1959, 1961a, 1961b, 1974) discussed "situated activity systems," in which he showed how people interacted and became part of their communities. In many very insightful studies, he also showed that "doing is being," an idea to which we shall return later in this chapter. In precisely the same manner, the well-known sociologist Karl Mannheim (1936) suggested that individuals do not always think innovative thoughts; rather, they "participate in thinking further what other [people] have thought before" (p. 3). Fellow practitioners may already have had similar ideas, reflecting on their own practice because they have experienced similar problems, and newcomers have to learn the history of their occupation, which will soon become their own.

In a similar manner to Lave and Wenger, Dreyfus and Dreyfus (1980) suggest that there are three stages in this process: from reliance on abstract principles to the use of concrete experience; from viewing the situation as a compilation of bits to seeing it as a whole; and from detached observer to involved performer. In other words, as the newcomers become socialized into the professional culture (Elliott, 1972), they become more fully involved practitioners. Accompanying this process is the movement from novice to expert, which Dreyfus and Dreyfus suggest goes through five stages, as a result of their studies with chess players and airline pilots:

1. Novice: beginners with no experience of the situation in which they are expected to perform

2. Advanced beginner: can demonstrate marginally acceptable performance

3. Competent: typified by someone who has been in the job for two or three years

4. Proficient: perceives situations as a whole rather than as pieces and whose performance is guided by experience

5. Expert: has an intuitive grasp of each situation and need not consider a vast range of alternative possibilities

This model is also appropriate to nursing, as Benner (1984) has demonstrated. We can see here how practitioners move from the rational legitimation of their knowledge to a pragmatic legitimation. Finally, with the experts, there is almost a tacit legitimation, since they take their expertise for granted.

Continuing practice, it appears, is a gradual movement from novice to expert. But not all long-serving practitioners are experts. Indeed, as companies are downsizing they are tending to treat older workers as if they were as obsolete as last year's calendar, although this might well be shown in the future to be a fundamental mistake. Benner (1984) does make the point, however, that not all novices will be able to become experts, so it is necessary to understand why some people do not progress all the way.

Habituation

An expert's practice is rather like the way most of us behave in everyday life, which Schutz and Luckmann (1974) describe in the following manner: "I trust that the world that has been known to me up until now will continue further and that consequently the stock of knowledge obtained from my fellow-men and formed from my own experiences will continue to preserve its fundamental validity. . . . From this assumption follows the further and fundamental one: that I can repeat my past successful acts" (p. 7). They are saying that our actions are habituated and will persist until something different occurs that prevents us from performing them. We all know this—indeed, social life is grounded on the expectations that people will act in a consistent manner. When we are confronted with disjuncture, however, we can no longer take things for granted, although most of us are happier when we can presume on our behavior. But habituation can have its dangers. In an influenza epidemic, a doctor treats many patients who describe precisely the same symptoms to him, to the point that while they are talking he begins to write the prescription and does not concentrate quite so much on what the patient is telling him. It is easy in that situation to miss something vital that a patient might include in the general description.

What processes do we go through to habituate our practice? In *Paradoxes of Learning* (Jarvis, 1992) I described a five-stage process through which our actions become habituated:

1. *Experimental or creative action*. Kelly's theory of human personality (1963) assumes that human behavior is rather like a scientific experiment where actors might well know what they are doing but neither the means nor the outcomes are assured beforehand. There is a need for careful planning, but even more significant, this is individualistic and stems from a situation where the external demands to conform are insufficiently great to inhibit new forms of action in the given circumstances. These forms of action might be slight adaptations to previously enacted behavior, or they might be entirely new.

2. *Repetitive behavior*. We have learned a way of performing an act, and every time the situation occurs, we try to repeat it in precisely the same way. This is how skillful behavior is learned, and it is the form of action that training often seeks to instill in practitioners.

3. *Presumptive action*. We act unthinkingly in a situation, as if it were instinctive, even though we know it is not because we have been through a learning process. Having reached this presumptive position, we are also in a nonlearning position. This is habituation.

4. *Ritualism*. This is the process of "going through the motions" because we no longer have to think about the situation, which can be dangerous both to practice and to ourselves as individuals. It is dangerous to practice because, like the doctor with the influenza patient, we might miss little differences that tell us the situation has changed, and it is dangerous to ourselves because we begin to act as automatons rather than as human beings.

5. *Alienation*. We act in a conforming manner but without meaning because we are powerless to change our behavior. *Alien-*

ation is the term that Karl Marx attached to the idea that repetitive work situations can destroy human creativity.

In a situation of disjuncture, when our experiences and biography do not match (see Chapter Four), we are unsure how to act; we are in an experimental or creative situation. We are doing something new, but as we become more familiar with it, the degree of disjuncture lessens and we repeat our actions and then presume on our situation. Like the doctor treating flu, ritualism sets in, and finally the actions no longer stimulate us at all. Working in boring, repetitive jobs, our actions become alienating and self-destructive. There is a significant relationship between the degree of disjuncture, which contains the potential for learning something new, and habituation. When I cease to learn from a situation, I have habituated to it, and it becomes repetitive and eventually alienating.

This process is quite natural—we all go through it—but significantly we can see how easy habituation of our actions becomes in Benner's stage of competency (1984), when we have been doing the same job for two or three years. Not all practitioners become experts, and even experts can easily presume on a changing situation and make mistakes. Indeed, the situation itself does play an important part in this process.

What makes experts experts is that they *problematize* their situations: they keep learning, even when it is easier to habituate and not learn. Expertise does not come naturally; it is a discipline of continually seeking improvement, which can require a great deal of effort. The experts are always operating in an experimental mode, even though their experience makes a work situation seem simple, and they adjust to changing circumstances with apparent ease.

Habitus

At the point when we begin to habituate our actions, we reach a plateau of knowledge, action, and feelings—our *habitus*, as Bourdieu (1990) calls it. Practitioners often feel comfortable in their social situations, fully socialized and experienced. That is why experienced practitioners can take their situation and their performance for granted. Bourdieu (1990, p.54) suggests that the "*habitus*, a product of history, produces individual and collective practices . . . in accordance with the schemes generated by history" (p. 54). Indeed, the habitus does not exist by itself—it can only exist because we are conscious of it and in our relationship with others who also practice within it. Indeed, the habitus does not just contain knowledge and skill, even in totally impersonal, individualized work situations; it is much wider. If, for instance, we think of nurses' or educators' fields of practice, the practitioners have attitudes, values, beliefs, and emotions about them, all learned from practicing. Thus the habitus is a complex culture, varying from one field of practice to another, lending itself to apparently spontaneous practice. In another sense, it might also restrict innovations and creativity if these are contrary to its history.

Bourdieu (1990) further suggests that "the *habitus*—embodied history, internalized as a second nature and so forgotten as history—is the active presence of the whole past of which it is a product. As such, it is what gives practices their relative autonomy with respect to external determinations of the immediate present." He goes on to suggest that "the *habitus* is a spontaneity without consciousness or will," so that we can presume on our experiences apparently without further thought. "The *habitus* which, at every moment, structures new experiences in accordance with the structures produced by past experiences which are modified by new experiences within the limits defined by their power of selection, brings about a unique integration, dominated by the earliest experiences, of the experiences statistically common to members of the same class" (pp. 56, 60). By "class" Bourdieu means category or group. The habitus is the integration of the culture of the organization or workplace and the experienced workers' understanding of how to perform their roles in their present situation. Individual practice is situated in the wider world, and the spontaneity is both constrained by and reinforced by the internalized structures and procedures. Nevertheless, practice is individual but situated. The habitus survives because it works. It adjusts itself in response to wider social changes, but only by responding to the pressures that reinforce it. It is a conservative phenomenon, reflexive only to a degree.

Consequently, when experienced workers advise interns to forget the theory they learned in college or university, it is because it is clearly not the theory that structures their daily performance; it is their habitus—the combination of their past; their own knowledge, skills, and understanding of the situation in which they function; their common discourse; and their confidence in the correctness of what they are doing. Implicit in their advice is that the interns need a different form of legitimation for their practice, stemming from both the experienced practitioners' own sense of belonging and their confidence that what they do works.

Doing and Being

In Chapter Four we defined *learning* as the process of creating and transforming experience into knowledge, skills, attitudes, values, beliefs, emotions, and senses. Learning is the process by which the whole person emerges, not merely parts. So far we have discussed only the first two elements—knowledge and skills—yet the remainder are also learned from the work experience.

When I used to teach a course in the sociology of work, I once asked about one hundred part-time adult students in a lecture class to respond to the question "Who am I?" by completing the sentence "I am (a) . . ." ten times. I said that I would not ask them to reveal their answers to anyone, although I would ask them one question about them. When they had completed their responses, I asked, "How many of you have put your occupation in the top three?" Nearly 70 percent of them had done so. They had learned to "be" their occupation—it had provided them with an identity. In the United States, the standard introduction is, "Tell us your name and what you do" or "I'd like you to meet Mrs. X, a financial consultant from Pennsylvania." You automatically are your occupation.

I still use this exercise when I lead preretirement sessions. When I have found out how many participants have included their occupational identity high on the list, I ask them who they are going to be when they retire.

Think back to the model of learning shown in Figure 4.1. A person enters a situation and creates an experience—the whole person. And it is the whole person who learns from it, who gains not only identity but also satisfaction, confidence, enjoyment, challenge, likes and dislikes, and so on. All of these elements interrelate with the practice we have described, perhaps indicating one reason that some people's skill levels plateau before others, since some are challenged by their situation while others are bored by it, some like it while others dislike it, and so forth. Consequently, some people feel that they need to get continuing education while others have no desire to continue; some seek to improve their practice and become experts while others are content at other levels in the novice-to-expert hierarchy. It is a reflexive system. We are all individuals, finding our places and acting within the larger system of the habitus.

Knowledge, skills, and habitus, however, are not always in accord. A few years ago, Kathy, a nurse educator, took a year of unpaid leave to return to university full-time to work toward a higher degree. During the year, she studied hard, gained a great deal of new knowledge, and undertook a small research project as a practitioner-researcher, from which she gained many new ideas. At the end of her year, she returned to her place of employment, fired with enthusiasm to try to introduce into her practice some of the things she had learned from her research project. When I asked her a few months later how she was getting on, she was despondent. Nothing had appeared to change while she was away; nothing she had learned was acceptable within the school. All she could do was make small adjustments to her own practice, which was not really as satisfying as she had anticipated. When I talked to her, she was about to seek new employment elsewhere.

On returning to her old job she had wanted to be a change agent (London, 1988), but she was prevented from introducing the changes she had hoped to introduce. I call this *preventative non-action* (Jarvis, 1992). It affected her job satisfaction, which reflected on her practice performance. She knew that unless she changed her place of employment, her whole being would be affected by what she could and could not do, despite the ideas she had gained from her stint as a practitioner-researcher.

Had the situation been different—had her managers been innovative or more permissive—Kathy's frustration might have been avoided. Unless whole units, departments, or organizations respond to the tremendous pressures to change, Kathy's experience will not be unusual. This is one reason that the concept of the learning organization is currently being promulgated (Watkins and Marsick, 1993).

The concept of the learning organization is fundamentally different from traditional theories of organizations. Max Weber (1947), a founding father of organizational analysis, suggested that "the management of the office follows general rules which are more or less stable, more or less exhaustive and can be learned" (Gerth and Mills, 1948, p. 148). In other words, Weber considered that practitioners should learn the rules and procedures of the organization nonreflectively and abide by them. Bureaucratic organizations are, almost by definition, prone to inertia. These are the very conditions that caused Kathy her distress.

It is also being recognized that bringing consultants into organizations to introduce change may be an effective way of continuing learning. Consulting roles in all occupations and professions will consequently continue expanding.

Conclusion

Even if the practice site was not changing, practicing is situated and is itself a unique and ever-changing performance. Though every situation is unique—the same water cannot flow under the same bridge twice—there are patterns on the water that appear to be the same. It is sometimes difficult, however, to recognize all the differences when the similarities appear on the surface. Bourdieu (1990) writes, "The theory of practice as practice insists, contrary to positive materialism, that the objects of knowledge are constructed, not passively recorded and, contrary to intellectual idealism, that the principle of this construction is the system of structured, structuring dispositions, the *habitus* which is constituted in practice and is always orientated towards practical functions. . . . To do this, one has to situate oneself *within* "real activity as such," that is in practical relation to the world" (p. 52). It is only through being involved with the practice, speaking the same language and understanding the situation, that it is possible to understand the complexities of every unique performance. It is in this context that the practitioner-researcher has emerged.

Reflective practice itself is a product of the same social processes, so it is necessary to examine this before we move on to look at the research role of the practitioner-researcher.

Chapter Six

Reflective Practice

Schön (1983) was correct to relate the rise of the reflective practitioner to the death of technical rationality; an era of reflexive modernity is dawning. In a similar way, Giddens (1990) has suggested that "modernity is constituted in and through reflexively applied knowledge but the equation of knowledge with certitude has turned out to be misconceived" (p. 39). Indeed, we have already shown this to be the case, but we still might wonder why there is such an emphasis on reflexivity at the present time. The answer lies partly in the fact that modernity has undergone such rapid transformation and fragmentation: the introduction of new manufacturing techniques and new information technologies, the shift from a manufacturing orientation to a service orientation, the trend toward regarding education and learning as commodities, and so forth. Everything seems to be changing; the expression "I don't know what the world is coming to these days" has never been more true. As things change, society is forced to confront the outcomes of these changes; in a sense, society itself is becoming reflexive. It is a learning society. It is a society that demands constant reexamination: the risk society demands more than reflectivity; it calls for constant research. The practitioner-researcher is a natural outcome of the risk society—this is a theme that we will return to in Part Four.

How does reflectivity relate to reflexivity? Beck (1994) seeks to distinguish the two by pointing out that reflexivity is a confrontation that fragmented society has with itself when the normal procedures for coping with change are unable to assimilate everything that is occurring, thereby generating risk. Reflection, by contrast, occurs within individuals when "the self is no longer just the un-equivocal self but has become fragmented into contradictory discourses of the self. Individuals are now expected to master these 'risky opportunities,' without being able, owing to the complexity of modern society, to make the necessary decisions on a well-founded and responsible basis, that is to say, considering the possible consequences" (p. 8).

Reflective practice, then, is a natural outcome of reflexive modernity. Nevertheless, does this not clash with the idea of the habitus, discussed in Chapter Five? Reflexive modernity has clearly weakened the power of the traditions, but they have not been destroyed.

Our purpose now is to examine this reflective practice, and we shall do so under four headings: reflectivity, disjuncture, reflective practice, and reflective practice and research.

Reflectivity

In recent years, the idea of reflective practice has been quite predominant in many professions, demonstrating the tremendous effect that Schön's writings have had on the field of practice. Nevertheless, many earlier thinkers (Dewey, 1916; Freire, 1972) have considered reflection an essential element in both thinking and learning. Even Aristotle wrote about the subject; he was perhaps the first person to do so. He suggested that "it is thought to be the mark of a man of practical wisdom to be able to deliberate well about what is good and expedient for himself" (1991, p. 142). He regarded as a virtue being "concerned with things human and things about which it is possible to deliberate" (p. 146). In a sense, Aristotle was writing about people who thought about the practical things of life; they were reflective thinkers possessed of practical reason.

But to understand the dynamics of this, it is necessary to extend our previous discussion of practical knowledge. There are two strands to this discussion, a psychological one and a sociological one. Dealing with the psychological first, we shall look at learning styles, which in turn relate to personality types.

Impulsivity Versus Reflectivity

People do not all think in the same way. In cognitive psychology, for instance, a distinction is drawn between thinkers who are impulsive and those who are reflective. Kagan (1971) suggested that among children, there are those, on the one hand, who "have a fast conceptual tempo; they impulsively report the first classification that occurs to them or carry out the first solution sequence that appears appropriate. The reflective children, on the other hand, characteristically delay before reporting or carrying out a solution hypothesis" (p. 37). Children do get more analytical as they get older, and they certainly have more experiences on which to base their judgments, but we can safely assume that these personality types do not disappear in adulthood.

Kagan goes on to make the point that reflective thinkers are not necessarily cautious; they simply prefer to consider more alternatives before they reach a solution. Likewise, some practitioners are more likely than others to consider a greater number of alternative strategies in their role performance.

This finding gives rise to two forms of practice other than habituation—impulsivity and reflexivity in practice—and these may be depicted as in Figure 6.1. Impulsive practitioners, having arrived at a solution to their problem, put it into practice, and they may not trouble to reflect on it thereafter, as the dotted lines in part (a) are meant to suggest. In contrast, reflective thinkers examine the alternatives and act accordingly, regarding their actions as experiments from which they can continue to learn, so that they both reflect in the action and continue to reflect after it—as the double arrow in part (b) indicates. This is what Schön (1983) regards as "reflection in action," a process of thinking about action in such a manner as to generate new knowledge, which will in turn generate new action, or vice versa.

The distinction between reflective and impulsive practice occurs in management consultancy. A consultant goes into a large company and confronts a problem, but one that he or she has faced

Figure 6.1. Impulsive and Reflective Practice Compared.

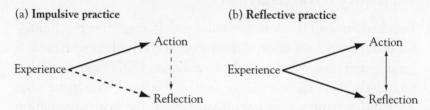

before in a very similar situation. It is beguilingly easy to fall back on this previous experience and "choose the most comfortable way—suggesting what he or she has done in similar situations with previous clients, or choosing the first solution that will come to mind" (Kubr, 1996, pp. 207, 209).

In a sense, these diagrams are just a restructuring of our original diagram about learning (Figure 4.1), since the impulsive practitioner is more likely to place more emphasis on doing and less on reflecting in the first instance, whereas the reflective practitioner initially places more emphasis on reflecting.

There is therefore a psychological component, a predisposition, in our understanding of reflective practice: we all decide for ourselves how to act, but in similar situations, different people act differently, according to their personality types.

The extent to which we can create reflective thinkers through simple training courses is therefore an open question, although some professions have introduced such courses into their professional preparation.

Habitus

Practice is affected by the wider social world, so we must examine the social dimension. Indeed, our habitus—our individual collection of knowledge, action, and feelings associated with a specific set of conditions—is social, and because people rarely work in total isolation, they are exposed to the social pressures that are operating in their social situations. This means that their experiences are also socially constructed, and to some extent so are the outcomes of their experiences. Thus the dynamics shown in Figure 6.1 can be expanded to incorporate the social dimension. Figure 6.2 shows these expanded dynamics for the reflective practitioner, who is more likely to be aware of the social pressures than the more impulsive practitioner is.

The circle represents the wider social world, and the opposing arrows depict something of the dialectical relationship between the practice situation and the wider world. It is not possible to isolate experiences and actions from these social pressures that surround the situation, so action is rarely free from some considerations about these forces. The social forces may be inconsequential for individuals of certain dispositions or those who exercise power, but for a number of practitioners working in organizations or with other people, the effects of their actions have to be considered. Or they may merely respond to the pressures and conform. For many others, however, perhaps even for most, there is a dialectical relationship between thinking about practice and thinking about the situation in which practice occurs (Lave, 1988).

Figure 6.2. The Social Dimension of Practice.

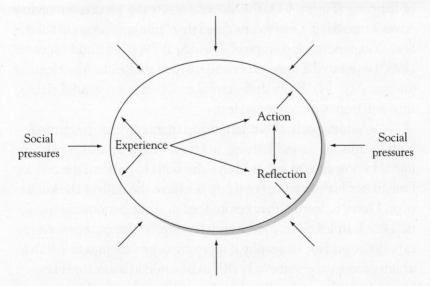

Disjuncture

Chapters Four and Five discussed our reliance on presumption—taken-for-granted tacit knowledge and habituated behavior. If we can do it and know how to do it, we can presume on our actions almost intuitively or unthinkingly. But there are times when I am unsure how to act. If, for instance, I were to go into a nuclear physics laboratory, I would not know where to begin, either to act or to learn, because the gap between my biography and my experience is so great that I would need many hours of study even to begin to understand the rudiments of the subject. By contrast, if I am asked a very difficult question about moral philosophy, I might be able to begin to reason out answers, or if I am called on to build a cupboard in my kitchen, I might have to practice my carpentry skills. The point is, in neither of the latter two cases can I act unthinkingly. In all three examples, however, there is a gap between my biography and my experience. In the first one, the gap is too large to be bridged easily, but in the other two, the gap can be closed with a little learning.

Disjuncture occurs when there is disharmony between my constructed experience of a situation and my biography—in the diagram of learning (Figure 4.1), this is once again the process involving boxes 1 through 3. Dewey considered that "thinking occurs when the flow of experience is disrupted" (Wirth, 1979, p. 86), and Mezirow (1990) refers to the same experience, which they call a "disorienting dilemma" (p. 14). Every disjunctural situation is a potential change situation from which one can learn.

It is, significantly, this relationship that is crucial to learning—both learning to do and learning to know. This is a paradox of learning: if I know how to act or I have the skills to perform the action, I might not learn from it, but if I do not have the skills or the knowledge, I have to learn either before I act or while performing the action itself. In learning, I grow and develop, so the gap between my experience and my biography is more important for my growth than a harmonious experience is. I call this situation a disjuncture between biography and experience; others have branded it a problem.

Hence more emphasis has been placed on problem-based learning, although the word *problem* has unfortunate undertones—people say, "No problem," implying that the more able people are, the less likely it is that they will experience problems, even though we know that this is simply not true. Having no problems might actually be dangerous. Yet part of the way successful people try to present themselves to the world is of having effortless superiority. This is an interesting paradox of our social life.

Problem-based action leads both impulsive and reflective practitioners to respond in their different ways to the situation, yet both might seem adequate and reflective on the surface. What happens when an action is successful? Should we never consider that success is also a "problem"? Do practitioners never need to ask why a success is a success? Perhaps this is another major difference between the reflective and the impulsive practitioner. The latter responds to problems, but the former is capable of being proactive and problematizing situations.

When I used to train teachers (both schoolteachers and educators in the professions), I would often talk with the students after observing them teach. I found that it was easy for them to tell me what had gone wrong with their lessons—they could easily begin to learn from these large disjunctures or problems that had occurred during class. When asked, however, to tell me about their successes during the lesson and to explain why they were successful, they found this much more difficult because they had not learned to problematize success. Problem solving is one way by which we learn in practice, but practical reason demands that we create our own disjunctures and pose problems for ourselves. The ability to pose problems is certainly as important as the ability to solve them, and it is only the reflective practitioners who engage in this form of practice.

This is what Argyris and Schön ([1974] 1992) called "double-loop learning": seeing that I have to learn to solve the problem, I have to problematize the situation in which the problem occurs or else I have to pose problems that are not necessarily apparent to the practice. In other words, I have to create disjuncture. Proactivity is as important a factor in this process as reactivity.

Problem posing means that reflective practitioners are not just responsive to the changing conditions of their practice; they are proactively asking questions about it. They create their own problems, or disjuncture, so they are agents as well as recipients of the forces of change, and as can be seen from the learning diagram, they can create new knowledge, attitudes, values, and skills for themselves by responding positively to potential learning situations. By so doing, they also stop the process of habituation in their performance, and there is a sense that by so doing, they disturb the habitus. Herein lies the basis of reflective practice.

Reflective Practice

Schön (1983) showed how practice has changed from technical rationality to reflection in action. He concentrated, rightly, on reflection in action, which he typified as the art of practice, although he recognized another approach to reflection, which he called a "postmortem." We have already noted, however, that reflective practitioners will also think and plan their strategies before they act, so we shall examine all three approaches: reflective planning; reflection in action, and retrospective reflection.

Reflective Planning

Reflective practitioners, especially those who are still climbing the expertise hierarchy, may need to spend more time on planning their strategies before they put them into action. As a manager, I would write notes about the strategy that I might deploy in a difficult situation that was likely to arise a couple of days ahead. Nearer the time, I would return to those notes, reconsider the ideas, and perhaps make amendments in the light of the situation. Professors, planning their lectures, might outline different strategies for their presentation a few days in advance and adopt one of them in the light of circumstances on the day. For example, not long ago, I had planned a presentation to a large group of students using small groups, but I had written the material as a lecture. Perhaps fifteen minutes before the session, I heard some of the students saying they were having far too many small group sessions and they were not really enjoying them—so I delivered the material as a lecture. When planning notes for sessions exist, practitioner-researchers would be wise not to throw them away, no matter how untidy the scraps of papers on which they are recorded may be.

Reflection in Action

For Schön (1983), practice is not a mindless application of rules and procedures but a dynamic, living art, changing with the ebb and flow of life but still constrained by the social context within which it is performed. Schön typifies certain aspects of this concept with the phrases "thinking on your feet" and "learning by doing." According to the first phrase, we learn from our thinking, and according to the second, we learn as we go; using the terminology discussed earlier, these might be the reflective and the impulsive ways of responding to the disjunctural situation.

For instance, an antiques expert is presented with a rare piece of silver—he looks for its date stamps, for the maker's name or mark, and for other clues about its manufacture. He might consult books and talk with colleagues, if he has time, but then he has to make a decision about the worth of the artefact. That decision will also depend to a considerable extent on his "feel" for the object. If he lacks the time to consult books or colleagues, he will have to make a valuation based on what he could see on the piece itself plus on his feel for it. He is thinking on his feet, and the greater his expertise, the more likely he is to rely tacitly on his feel for the object.

Similarly, an expert nurse might know right away the best way to respond to a patient who is suffering extremely painful symptoms. Asked why she gave the patient the treatment she did, she might reply that she "just knew" it was the best course of action.

By contrast, the impulsive practitioner might be confronted with a problem, immediately see a solution, and try it out—only to find that it does not work, so he has to begin the process of solving the problem all over again.

Reflection in action is the process of experimentation; it is creative and demands retrospection as well.

Retrospective Reflection

When I worked in a college of education and went to visit student schoolteachers doing their teaching practice, I always asked them for their notes on every lesson they had taught since I last saw them. They would often produce a large file, even though I was expected to see them twice a week. The file would be filled with notes about the lesson (both content and process), the audiovisual aids they used, and their evaluation of the lesson. I did not always have time to work through the many pages of notes they had prepared, but I always read all of their lesson evaluations—their retrospective reflections on their lessons. I was interested to see what went right and what went wrong—and their understanding of both. As I intimated earlier, I often asked them about what went right because they rarely included this in their evaluations. They were then encouraged to try out the results of their reflections in subsequent lessons. Evaluating their practice was a major learning experience—not as important as teaching the lesson, but very important if they were to become expert teachers.

In all of these forms of reflection, practitioners acquire more practical knowledge and more skill, which are their own. Practice is both a site and an opportunity for learning, and reflective practice is a necessary approach to learning how to become an expert practitioner. The results of reflection can then be used in planning for future action—what management consultants call "action planning" (Kubr, 1996).

Reflective Practice and Research

At the end of *The Reflective Practitioner*, Schön (1983) also raised issues about how the reflective practitioner could be a researcher. *Research* might be defined as "systematic investigation to establish facts or principles"; "systematic investigation to collect information on a subject"; or "investigations into a subject or problem" (*Collins English Dictionary*, 1979). It is clear from these definitions that reflection might be seen as a kind of individual and subjective research process—establishing principles, gathering more information about problems, and so on. In precisely the same way, it might be argued that practitioner-researchers are actually reflective practitioners, because they research their own practice and, of necessity, must reflect on it.

Schön (1983) highlighted four ways that reflective practitioners might engage in "reflective research":

- *Frame analysis*. When practitioners become aware of their "frames," they become aware of alternatives that might lead to further reflection in action about their own practice.
- *Repertoire-building research*. This serves the function of accumulating and describing useful examples of reflection in action. It is the use of case study in law, but it varies from profession to profession.
- *Research on fundamental methods of inquiry and overarching theories*. Schön sees two ways in which this might occur: first, by examining episodes of practice that may help others entertain different ways of thinking and seeing; and second, action science, which is concerned with situations of uniqueness, uncertainty, and instability (Argyris, Putnam, and Smith, 1985).
- *Research on the process of reflection in action*. By seeking to understand their practice, practitioners could restructure it.

Because Schön was starting with the reflective practitioner, it is not surprising that he focused specifically on ways of researching reflective practice. All of these would be included in any list of topics that practitioner-researchers might research. It would be possible, however, by reviewing the earlier chapters of this book, to extend this list to many aspects of their practice, all of which might also be viewed as reflections on their practice.

For instance, among the topics that practitioner-researchers might research are

- The changing nature of their practice
- The relationship between professional preparation and practice
- The way practitioners develop their practical knowledge
- The development of expertise
- Habituation and tacitness
- The effects of the habitus
- The development of professional identity
- The interrelationship between levels of expertise and identity, satisfaction, and so on
- The relationship between practice and continuing education

This list is by no means exhaustive, but it does point to the fact that reflective practice comes close to the role a practitioner-researcher performs. This view is also recognized by McNiff (1988), who relates reflective practice to action research.

Conclusion

Practice can be characterized as unique, transitory, individualistic (in terms of knowledge, skills, and reasoning), habituating, tacit, and patterned. Practitioners are involved in unique transitory events that engage whole persons and their situations. Their practice is unique to themselves but constantly interacting with their habitus in a reflexive society.

For practitioner-researchers, the problem is how to study such ephemeral phenomena and how such studies can be used to improve the practice and theory of their chosen profession. In Part Three we briefly look at some of the types of research that might be employed, and in Part Five we examine some of the implications of our discussions.

Part Three

Research in Practice

Chapter Seven

Case Studies

Practitioner-researchers are researchers. In Part Three I look at the research methods that are most appropriate to their work. I outline some methodological considerations in five brief chapters, though I must stress that this book is not intended as a research methods guide for practitioner-researchers. Because they perform a dual role, practitioner-researchers are almost inevitably going to research their practice or their work situation, and the approaches for work-based research are limited. I have chosen to examine only those approaches that occur most frequently in the work of the practitioner-researchers with whom I work.

Practice is, as was concluded in Chapter Six, a unique situation: every person's practice constitutes an individual event each time it happens. Consequently, it must be studied through individual cases. Stake (1994, p. 238) makes the point, however, that "uniqueness . . . is not universally loved" by researchers. But I would suggest that this is not the case with practitioner-researchers. At least one professional group has actually built the principle of uniqueness into its own practice: Nadler and Hibino (1994) point out that "whatever the apparent similarities, each problem is unique and requires an approach that dwells initially on its own contextual needs." Every consultation is an individual case, and every problem is unique, regardless of apparent similarities; this is the overt basis of management consultancy practice. Similarly, the case study must be the main means that practitioner-researchers employ in seeking to research these ephemeral events.

This chapter has three sections: the first examines the idea of a case study, the second probes the functions of case studies, and the third section considers the research reliability of case studies. It concludes with a brief discussion of the extent to which it is possible to generalize from the particular.

Case Studies: What Are They?

There are probably as many definitions of case studies as there are writers about them, which is not unusual in academic debate. No definition will gain universal agreement, although I provide an operational one shortly. Stake (1994) makes the point that both the words *case* and *study* raise questions in their own right. Significantly, Cohen and Mannion (1985) do not include practitioner-conducted action research in their discussion of the case study, suggesting that case studies are restricted to investigations in which the researcher is either a participant or a nonparticipant observer. Collaborative research, which might include the practitioner, however, falls within their definition. In trying to differentiate approaches to research, they appear a little inconsistent.

Stake (1994) suggests that customarily people are cases and that situations can be cases, but processes are not because the actual process of practicing lacks the boundedness to be considered a case. This separation of practitioners from their practices strikes me as artificial. Indeed, one might ask how it is possible to conduct classroom research (Cross and Steadman, 1996) without reference to the process.

To my mind, there can be no practice without the practitioners; their innermost feelings, values, beliefs, and sense of identity constitute part of the practice, so to omit these dimensions is to distill out some of the richness of the actual practice event. Throughout my own research into human learning, I have always argued that individual learning constitutes the basis of human biography and that every learning event is biographical. Therefore, if we are to understand practitioners' learning and practical reasoning, we must include in the case study both the practitioners and the processes by which they learn and practice.

Of course, this whole argument seems specious when you realize that central to our understanding of practitioner-researchers and their role is that they do conduct research into their own practice, and because their practice is transitory, they can only conduct case studies.

Expanding on Stake's definition of a case study as "the process of learning about the case and the product of our learning" (1994, pp. 236–237), I suggest that case studies are both about the *process* of learning about and researching the specific phenomenon or phenomena under investigation and about the *product* of that learning and research. Although I might claim here that research case studies are conducted primarily by practitioner-researchers in relation to their own practice, I acknowledge that other case studies are conducted in collaboration with others or even by researchers without references to practitioners at all.

Case studies are not always research. Often they constitute the practice itself. For instance, a case conference or case study is convened when social workers, community workers, and medical and educational personnel meet to discuss a problem family in order to draw up a report for a court of law. On other occasions, such conferences are used for teaching purposes—sometimes they are true events, but sometimes they are specifically devised for the purpose. For instance, Cross and Steadman (1996) record a case study devised by Jerry Evensky of Syracuse University about "the Leslies." The hypothetical story begins with an e-mail from a teacher of economics to a colleague in the chemistry department asking whether the second teacher has had similar problems to hers. The problem involves an intelligent woman student studying economics but not understanding any of it, getting D grades all the time, despite working very hard and doing well in other subjects. She does not understand the mathematics, it is clear that she has a mental block about the subject, so she wants to drop economics. The teacher does not want her to drop it because she believes that this woman is typical of the students she ought to be reaching, and she also does not want other students finding themselves in a similar position and dropping out. The colleague's response is supportive but clearly recognizes that the student might be better off dropping the subject, so the second e-mail indicates that the chemistry teacher would support the student's request to drop economics because she does not have the necessary knowledge to understand the math. She goes on to talk about pretesting. The third e-mail records the economics teacher saying that she supported the student dropping the course, and the student promising that she would go to the math department and get more math and then return to the economics class. The final e-mail is of the teacher saying that she had arranged for pretests for her economics students in the future to avoid having other students end up in the same situation.

Practitioner-researchers conduct case study research that may be used for teaching or management purposes, or that may even be published in order to get a wider critical audience for the research undertaken. At the moment, however, a great deal of practitioner research remains unknown to the wider world because it might not have been treated as valid research, so it can be discovered only within the pages of theses and dissertations hidden away in university libraries. These are consulted occasionally by others who are looking for the same type of information—it is what Bourdieu (1993) describes as writing for other creators rather than for the wider market. This should change as practitioner research becomes more widely recognized.

Functions of Case Studies

Let us explore this theme of usefulness a little further. Guba and Lincoln (1981, p. 372), for instance, suggest that there are four reasons for undertaking case studies:

- Chronicling: to record the salient steps in the process
- Rendering: to describe what it is like to experience the situation

- Teaching: to acquaint students with role expectations
- Testing: experimentation

Merriam (1988, pp. 11–12) suggests four similar reasons for case studies, describing them as:

- Particularistic: specific
- Descriptive: as full a description as can be recorded
- Heuristic: illuminating the phenomenon under study
- Inductive: not providing a generalized account that can be applied in a deductive manner

We can see that Lincoln and Guba and Merriam broadly agree on the functions of case studies, although Merriam is less concerned with the experimental and also omits the idea of rendering, but she might see this as part of her heuristic function.

If we look at these points, we can see that chronicling the steps in the process (the descriptive function) is important, and it is possible to see how the economics teacher went through a number of steps:

1. Diagnosing the student's weakness
2. Interviewing the student
3. Seeking advice
4. Reinterviewing the student
5. Contacting other expert interested parties
6. Devising a strategy for the future

I have already noted that management consultants see their work as being with unique cases, and it is interesting that the five stages in their process—entry, diagnosis, action planning, implementation, and termination (Kubr, 1996)—are very similar to the six listed here. To describe what it is like to experience the situation (rendering/heuristic), it is necessary for the researcher to get very close to the actors or for the practitioners to be the researchers. For instance, in recent months, I have been working with a newly established business school that has sought to produce a new taught master's degree on a part-time basis for practicing management consultants. To get the degree launched, it was decided that it would be wise to enter into collaboration with an established university. At the time when the approach was made, my university was already having a few difficulties with another external institution, although not about a collaborative arrangement of the type being proposed here. Despite the fact that the established university was extremely supportive of this partnership venture, it had never before entered such an arrangement and was very wary, partly because of its experience with the other organization and partly because of the innovative nature of the arrangement. Consequently, the university moved very slowly toward the collaborative agreement, costing the business school a lot of money and time, as well as a possible lead in the market for masters' degrees in management consultancy. It was also very frustrating for some of the people involved. After many months of negotiation, an agreement was hammered out, and new university procedures for validating the degree and new course regulations had been devised as a result of examining all the issues in this collaborative arrangement. The course is now about to be launched. One of the university administrative staff assured me that no similar arrangement in the future would take so long, thanks to all the work that had gone into this venture. Indeed, the process was unique and can never be repeated.

In this instance, the case study, which is as yet incomplete, reveals the dynamics of the organizations and the intricate problems that have to be overcome in such partnership arrangements. It also enables us to record the actual emotions of some of the actors, who were at times frustrated by the slowness of the developments.

None of the case studies here have been devised specifically as experiments, although many action research projects are implemented for this reason. Merriam (1988) makes a distinction between experimental and nonexperimental case studies, and Stake (1994) makes a similar distinction between intrinsic and instrumental ones. What I have been describing so far clearly relates to nonexperimental or intrinsic cases. Indeed, I have suggested that the site of practice is a laboratory and that practice is an act or an experiment, but this does not mean that the case study is experimental in itself. There is a fundamental difference between practice as experiment and the research being experimental. Once we build into the practice additional experimental elements, we cease to study the practice itself and study the changes that we are introducing. I am by no means attacking the nature of experiment here; obviously there is a major role for it. But its role in helping us to understand practice itself is limited. In another sense, every practice situation is an experiment because it has never occurred before, so the practitioners are responding to unique situations. Case studies about practice are, however, basically intrinsic.

There is a further reason for conducting case studies. Practitioner-researchers might be enabled to formulate hypotheses for future research, because research is becoming a more iterative process. Cross and Steadman (1996) note, for instance, that studying their cases enabled them to formulate hypotheses for future research.

Finally, Guba and Lincoln (1981) record why they feel that the case study is more beneficial than a technical report. This is important for practitioner-researchers who are sometimes required to make such reports to mangers. The case study provides

- "Thick description," with details as complete and as literal as possible
- Grounding—an experiential perspective
- Holistic and realistic (lifelike) perspectives
- A simplified range of data, without losing its integrity
- Illuminated meaning
- More in-depth communication than propositional language can provide

These echo the fundamental points that I have been making about the nature of practice from the outset of this book. Practice is personal and holistic and cannot be divided by discipline. One further point, however, can be added to these six: the technical report conveys the impression that the data provide scientific evidence of an empirical phenomenon called practice, rather than a record of a transitional human event that cannot ever be repeated in precisely the same manner.

Practitioner-researchers are able to provide qualitative evidence about the complex, transitory, and human nature of practice. But is their research merely anecdotal?

The Reliability of Case Studies

Guba and Lincoln (1981) suggest that case studies do have a number of disadvantages, including oversimplification, exaggerations of the facts, and interpretations of selective facts; they are unscientific, opportunistic, and unrepresentative; and they are partial accounts masquerading as full accounts. These objections deserve examination. All reports, of whatever kind, are representations or interpretations of some form of event or reality. It would be impossible to find any account that is not an oversimplification, but an example would be the summary of the partnership arrangement between the university and the business school given earlier. To trust the data completely would require a full record of every document drafted and every negotiation along the way. This has not been provided, and it would be impossible to document all the issues and all the people involved. The same is true of classroom research: it would be impossible to record all the parts each member of the class plays in a practice situation, to record every aspect of their emotions, feelings, attitudes, and so on. Reports are always partial accounts, even though they may sometimes give an impression of being more comprehensive than they are. Consequently, case studies are always going to be oversimplifications of the complexities of practice, no matter how conscientiously practitioner-researchers document them. We must not claim for case studies greater validity than we can demonstrate. If the research methods employed are rigorous, there is no reason to conclude that they are unscientific. Consequently, they need not be exaggerations. Admittedly, they are not representative, but the whole point of this discussion is that because practice is transitory it is not possible to get a scientific representative sample of practice, so studies must always be interpretations of selective facts and must necessarily be partial.

Even so, case studies have to be considered by criteria similar to those applied to other research. Traditionally, research projects have to have both internal and external validity. Internal validity means that it has to reflect the reality of the situation at hand, and external validity refers to the extent to which the findings can be studied in other situations. I am suggesting here that case studies do require internal validity but, because of the uniqueness of the practice event, it is not possible to provide external validity.

Internal Validity

Earlier in the book, I tried to show the problem of treating practice as though it were an empirical phenomenon. It is not one. For the purposes of research, it should not be treated as if it were. Every practice event is unique and ephemeral, and there is no empirical reality that can be carefully measured, checked, and rechecked; consequently, the reliability of the findings can be assessed only in relation to the methods used to gain the data in the first place. Therefore, the processes of observing, interviewing, and recording become very important. Provided that they are sufficiently rigorous, well planned, and undertaken in the most professional manner, something of their reliability has to be admitted.

The question then arises, however, about how the data are recorded. Because the data are descriptive, it might well be argued that the best way of presenting them is factually, without bias, and letting the readers make their own interpretation of what they see, read, or hear. The implications of this are that the practitioner-researcher has recorded the data and prepared them for presentation in a completely objective manner, attempting only to try to "tell the story" and letting the facts speak for themselves. This is not a possible undertaking, however, as Van Maanen (1988) has shown. He suggests that there are at least several different styles of presentation, all of which will influence the way that the recipient interprets the data—he describes these as interpreting realistically, impressionistically, confessionally, critically, formally, literarily, and jointly.

The act of preparing the presentation is always a political event in itself. Practitioner-researchers are naturally always going to ensure that any research report for management is going to contain the right tone, even if the data are not necessarily what management are seeking. In this sense, no meaningful research about practice can ever be presented in a value-free manner. Gadamer (1976) regards the prejudices of the presenters as natural. He has written that "prejudices are not necessarily unjustified and erroneous, so that they inevitably distort the truth. In fact, the historicity of our existence entails that prejudices, in the literal sense of the word, constitute the initial directedness of our whole ability to experience. Prejudices are biases to our openness to the world. They are simply conditions whereby we experience something—whereby what we encounter says something to us" (p. 9).

Interpreting the data is part of the hermeneutic process. Indeed, it is part of everybody's experience, so it does not matter whether we are dealing with a case study or with any other form of report; we still need to interpret it to get at the reality behind what is recorded.

External Validity

Merriam (1988) notes but does not agree with the fact that external validity is concerned with "the extent to which the findings of one study can be applied to other situations" (p. 173). Here we see the nature of the problem dealt with in this book: the practitioner-researchers' own practice is unique, so the findings from practice situations cannot be applied to other situations. The nature of practice dictates that we are concerned with the specific. There may well be similarities within unique and transitory practices, as the concept of habitus implies, but this is not an essential criterion for the validity of all case studies.

It might be argued that the inability to generalize from a case study means that it cannot have external validity. My position is that the criterion of external validity cannot be proved to be valid in itself, because every practice situation is different. Consequently, I must conclude that there are no criteria of external validity in case studies about practice.

Does this mean that the other criteria of research do not apply? I have already suggested that case study research, because it cannot be replicated, needs to be most rigorous. If it is anecdotal, it will be invalid.

Conclusion

The practitioner-researcher's research situation is always a particular situation, and for this reason it can be researched only as a case study. Stake (1994, p. 238) suggests six aspects of uniqueness:

- The nature of the case
- Its historical background
- The physical setting
- Other contexts, including economic, political, legal and aesthetic
- Other cases through which this case is recognized
- Informants through whom the case can be known

Not all of these aspects are applicable to every practice, but it can be seen from the illustrations in this chapter that the business school example is about a unique situation having a very particular historical background. In the business school–university collaboration, the business school is a unique player because it had no students, no premises of its own in the first instance, and few staff—unlike almost any other school. In the classroom research illustration, however, the case can be recognized because it rings true to many teachers' classroom experiences. Nevertheless, uniqueness does raise questions about the usefulness of case studies in the wider context.

This is rather like the old maxim, "The same water cannot flow under the same bridge twice." That is true. But if you stand on the bridge, you will see that different molecules of water make similar patterns—and we recognize that patterns of behavior do occur. Indeed, try to think about living in society if we cannot anticipate, on the basis of patterns of experience, how other people are going to respond to us. At the heart of social living are similarities and patterns. Perhaps this is why we find it so much easier to look for similarities and repetitions than to look for differences.

Consider again the case studies referred to in this chapter: the economics teacher wanted to find examples from similar situations, but the university–business school collaboration laid ground rules for other such arrangements precisely because there had never been any before. Indeed, I noted the similarities between the way the class teacher approached her colleague for advice and Kubr's five stages of consultation.

It would be inconceivable to think about social living without expecting patterns: we go into a store and know how to play the customer role, as students we enter a classroom and know where to sit, and so on. In the same way that there are patterns of behavior in everyday life, there might, but need not, be similarities between the forms of practice; we saw in our discussion of habitus that similarities might occur—but we cannot predict which elements of practice will be similar and which will be different.

Patterns of practice emerge and will be revealed within the uniqueness of each case study.

This chapter has indicated that because practice is transitory, the case study is the most reliable way of studying it. The case study itself can be studied as part of our knowledge of practice, but it can only record and illuminate things that have already happened. Such cases can be used for teaching purposes, but they do not provide knowledge that is to be applied in a deductive manner. The ideas, however, might be useful for practitioners to use in inductive and creative ways, assisting them to build their own body of practical knowledge. The findings might be useful for managers in the decision-making process, but they do not promise that the managerial decision will necessarily be correct simply because the findings are based on research.

Case studies form part of the knowledge of practice of any occupational group—part of its "body of knowledge"—but they are conducted in totally different ways. Some of them are briefly examined in the following chapters.

Chapter Eight

Action Research

Practitioner-researchers research their own practice: they know what works for them, and they are comfortable with their own body of practical knowledge and their own skills and attitudes about their practice. Practitioner research is increasingly becoming known as action research, a form of research that really began in education, although it has now spread to other professions.

McNiff (1988) reminds us that in the United States, Schwab (1969) was the initiator of classroom research (see Cross and Steadman, 1996). In the United Kingdom, Stenhouse (1975) was among the first to write about the practitioner as researcher when he suggested that schoolteachers should also be their own researchers. The reason he proposed this approach was that the classroom is a laboratory and teachers implementing a curriculum have to translate it into their own practice. He went on to suggest that each classroom is unique, so teachers have to work out their own practice in their own classroom. He argued that it "is not enough that teachers' work should be studied: they need to study it themselves" (p. 143). In a sense, he was arguing for self-directed research, and this has been quite a dominant point, as we shall see later in this chapter.

Schwab and Stenhouse, it will be recalled, were writing before the ideas of reflective practice began to gain currency and even before the idea that theory should be applied to practice was being widely questioned. For Stenhouse, the classroom is the laboratory, and teachers have to experiment in implementing a theoretical curriculum document. They have to devise for themselves the best way of putting it into practice. In other words, he was suggesting that in the curriculum implementation phase, schoolteachers are always acting in an experimental or creative manner such that the disjuncture between the practitioners' biographies and experience is most likely to result in further learning. They have to experiment with their practice and learn from it so they can devise a form of practice that works for them and build up their own body of knowledge about their own ways of doing things.

How are schoolteachers to use the curriculum? Is it a document they have to translate into practice through deduction or something to be used creatively and inductively? Policymakers may often expect documents to be used in a more deductive manner, although expert practitioners might be much more creative about it.

Teachers' patterns of role performance (teaching) are rarely, however, dependent on any specific curriculum, seeing that their practical expertise has come from having learned about the teaching process throughout the whole of their teaching career. Nevertheless, in being expected to do something different, in implementing a new curriculum, it is more difficult for habituated practice to occur. Teachers are therefore in a position to reflect on their teaching process, study it, and record their own reflections, attitudes, emotions, and so on.

Action research differs a little from reflective practice and has a number of definitions, but perhaps the description by Carr and Kemmis (1985) is among the most all-embracing: "Action research is simply a form of self-reflective enquiry undertaken by participants in social situations in order to improve the rationality and justice of their own practices, their understanding of these practices, and the situations in which the practices are carried out" (p. 162). Action research and reflective practice are very close to each other, and at times they may be simultaneous activities. Practitioner-researchers and action researchers might have different orientations, however.

To illustrate the implications of the discussions on action research for practitioner-researchers, this chapter has four brief sections on action research: differing orientation, differing location, processes, and strengths and problems. The chapter concludes with a brief reference to participant observation, a needed skill in the practitioner-researcher's repertoire.

Differing Orientations

Action research has, by definition, two different emphases: *action* (practice orientation) and *research* (research orientation). Although I prefer to draw this distinction, some writers on action research combine the two emphases. McNiff (1988, p. 4) suggests four reasons that schoolteachers should be action researchers:

- To improve education through change
- To encourage teachers to be aware of their own practice
- To be critical of that practice
- To be prepared to change it

Note that the first and last functions relate directly to practice and the middle two place more emphasis on the research.

Similarly, Cohen and Mannion (1985, pp. 209–210) suggest that there are eight diverse but overlapping situations in which action research can be used:

- Spur to action
- Personal functioning, human relations, and morale
- Job analysis
- Organizational change
- Planning and policymaking
- Innovation and change
- Problem solving
- Developing theoretical knowledge

They place more emphasis on the research orientation of action research than McNiff does. Many of the emphases that Cohen and

Mannion place on action research suggest that it need not always be individualistic but may be collaborative; we shall return to this in the next chapter.

We should accept that practitioner-researchers will be involved in both aspects of action research, although I would hesitate to claim that more emphasis should be placed on one or other orientation. The reasons for the research will determine the appropriate emphasis. If the research is conducted at the request of management, the immediate emphasis is almost certainly not going to be placed on change. A nurse undertaking her own action research into her practice might be endeavoring to improve her practice by what she is doing. But because she is working in a large organization, there may be procedures that inhibit change.

Some situations can have either emphasis. For instance, in the example of the university entering into collaboration with the management consultancy business school, the location becomes a potentially good action research project of this kind: either one where the participants sought to change university procedures to adapt to contemporary situations, or one where the participants were more interested in recording the process for posterity.

Differing Locations

Practice is a laboratory. This is perhaps the single most important thing practitioners have to recognize, whatever their occupation. Their practice is and always should be an experiment, creative rather than presumptive. Practitioners know what they are doing better than anybody else does.

Schoolteachers, however, teach their classes alone, and it is easier for them to innovate and to research their own practice than it is for practitioners such as nurses who work in teams, even though the issues might be openly discussed as part of the culture of practice. But innovation would nevertheless be easier in these situations than where practitioners work in tightly controlled bureaucratic organizations where procedures are strictly enforced.

For professionals who work relatively independently, or in a professional culture that does not inhibit them too greatly, their practice can be a learning practice. Those who are inhibited by the culture of the organization or by the social pressures of the workplace may find experimentation much more difficult or considerably slower. Even in these latter situations, reflective practitioners' practice can still be a laboratory, although the nature of the research might change. Indeed, the *location* of practice becomes the laboratory rather than the practice itself, and the practitioners might become researchers of organizational processes, change agents, or even agents seeking to slow down the process of change.

Two situations emerge, therefore: practice as laboratory and location of practice as laboratory. But practice is always a laboratory.

Action Research Processes

Kurt Lewin (1947) is generally regarded as the founder of action research, and he postulated three stages after the original idea or the initial question: planning, fact finding, and implementation. He recognized that action research is an iterative process—the fact finding modifies the original idea, which in turn requires more fact finding, and so on—until the findings are ultimately implemented. For Lewin, action research was action-oriented—to introduce change.

Action research is not necessarily practitioner-oriented; it was and still can be a form of research in which outside researchers intervene to effect change in practice. Peters (1997), however, makes the point that a great deal of action research is participatory and even collaborative—a point to which we will return in the next chapter.

McNiff (1988) describes a similar threefold process—planning, practicalities, and implications—which she then subdivides. For planning, the first questions are "What is your concern?" "Why are you concerned?" and "What can you do about it?" All of these points can also reflect a self-directed, reflective practitioner orientation to this approach to participatory action research. The planning might, however, stem from a manager's concern rather than from the practitioner who undertakes the research; it might also arise from the fact that a professor is working with practitioner-researchers who have work-based projects that require research, and so on.

The main issue for practitioner-researchers is precisely determining the research question. This is the crucial first stage: focusing on the question and analyzing its implications. After analyzing it, it is important to consider the available literature on the topic. A few years ago, Eisner (1984) observed, "Practitioners seldom read the research literature. . . . Even when they do, this literature contains little that is not so qualified or so compromised by competing findings, rival hypotheses, or faulty design that the framework could scarcely be said to be supported in some way by reasonable research" (p. 258). Practitioners seldom read the research literature because it was not written for them—it was written for other researchers, and that it why the competing research concerns were uppermost in the minds of the authors. Practitioner-researchers should be able to deal with some of this more obscure literature as they refine their own research question; furthermore, an increasing number of practitioner journals present the results of action research projects that practitioner-researchers may find useful.

As the question is refined, then, the practicalities of the research emerge:

- What data does the question demand that the practitioner-researchers obtain?
- Are they to be drawn only from their own practice?
- What other form of data collecting should they engage in?
- What are the cost and time implications?
- Are there ethical implications?

These questions can be elaborated on using textbooks about research. Once they have been answered, data collection can proceed, the data must be analyzed, and the research should be written up so that the findings can be shared with others.

Thus the process of action research for practitioner-researchers can be summarized as follows:

1. Specify and refine the research question.
2. Consult the relevant literature to help refine the research question.
3. Undertake the actual research. (This might run parallel to the literature search; because practitioner-researchers are actually practicing at the same time, the process of practicing will also assist in refining the question.)
4. Analyze the data.
5. Implement the findings and disseminate them.

This process is strikingly close to the process of consulting (Kubr, 1996).

1. Entry: initial entry into a company, discovering the problem
2. Diagnosis: diagnosing the problem and discovering the data
3. Action planning: developing possible solutions
4. Implementation: putting solutions in place
5. Termination: withdrawal, evaluation and follow-up

Management consultancy is an action-based profession, so the process is clearly oriented to an action outcome. As it gains its own body of knowledge, we might see an increasing concern toward the research orientation. Nevertheless, different professional groups will have slightly different approaches to their action research, although the overall process will no doubt always be similar. This approach is not free, however, of problems of which practitioner-researchers need to be aware.

Strengths and Problems

In my earlier analyses of practice, I noted that it is a transitory phenomenon in which the practitioners are an integral part of their practice. They are doing, thinking, and experiencing, all simultaneously. Video can record their actions but not their thinking or experiencing. They can, to some extent, record their own thinking and experiencing after the event in diaries and journals or on audiotape, although subsequent recording loses a little of the potency of the actual experience. They are also in a position to assess the amount of learning they have gained as a result of the experiences they have had. They can further evaluate whether their new knowledge and skills work for them on subsequent occasions.

In addition, when they are looking a little more widely at their practice, they are more likely to understand what occurs in practice than an outsider coming into the situation to assess it. Herein lies one of the outside researchers' or consultants' difficulties, for in this sense they are not insider practitioner-researchers. Practitioner-researchers are more likely to be in a position to pose the right questions for research than individuals coming from outside to investigate on a small-scale basis.

Even so, Sanford (1981) notes that no form of action research has been generally regarded as part of the mainstream social science research tradition. He goes on to point out that this is because the social sciences have concentrated on the academic disciplines, whereas the concern of action research is multidisciplinary. As I have argued throughout this book, practical knowledge is integrated rather than multidisciplinary, and the very concept of practical knowledge calls into question the validity of some of the mainstream social science research. Even so, this failure to be accepted indicates that there might still be some difficulties with viewing action research as research.

Indeed, there are at least seven problems that have to be faced if expert practitioner-researchers are to research their own practice.

1. Practitioner-researchers may not necessarily be able to describe precisely what they do, feel, or think about their practice. Experts might be experts in their practice, but watching, or recording on audiotape or videotape, might be a more accurate way of

recording it than trying to get the experts to detail what they do, know, and feel in an action research report about their role performance. Observation does not, however, record their intentions, their problems, and so on, and the interpretations that others place on the events may be far less accurate.

2. Recall that one major element of practical knowledge is tacit knowledge and that the processes of habituation and taken-for-grantedness come into play. Practitioners may not be consciously aware of precisely what they do in such a manner as to be able to detail it accurately. Neither might they always be consciously aware of being and becoming a practitioner. As Nyiri (1988) noted, experts' tacit knowledge can be such that they find it extremely difficult to articulate what they know. Consequently, what is recorded might actually omit some of the most significant aspects of individual practice—the routine knowledge, skills, attitudes, and so on of the experts' practice. Action research might be especially appropriate for examining instances in which experts are dealing consciously with a problem. In such situations, it is much more difficult to act presumptively; practitioners have to reflect and to act in a more experimental manner and to learn new things. They are much more aware of their feelings and attitudes. In these instances, performance is more conscious, and expert practitioners might be in a better position than other researchers to record in a diary or journal the process of reflection and change. Diary research, however, does have all the problems of recording actions after the event, when espoused theory may not match theory in action. Practitioners will record only the aspects of their practice that they recall when they are writing in their diary, and that may be quite some time after the event.

3. Practitioner-researchers are not necessarily expert researchers. Indeed, they are practitioners, not researchers, even if they are aware of what they do. They might not be able to write what they do in an academic discourse or to contextualize it within a broader framework.

4. Playing more than one role at the same time is always a problem. Practitioner-researchers who define themselves primarily as

practitioners may become self-conscious in practice situations. It is in practice that they have gained their sense of their identity as professionals, and they have constructed their practical knowledge on the basis of their own understanding of their abilities, predispositions, and other aspects of their practice. This knowledge is uniquely theirs, and they view practice from their own unique perspective. Trying to see themselves as researchers as well alters their role identity, and this immediately affects the way they approach and perform their practice role. The practice site changes to one for practice and research; now they have two roles, and they may not perform their practice role in the way they would if they were not also performing the research role.

5. Ethical issues also arise because practitioner-researchers are dealing with their colleagues and clients as practitioners. Should they, in the researcher role, use their colleagues or clients as subjects for research? One of my doctoral students, who is researching her own practice, said that there were times when she had to restrict her research because even though she wanted to ask her clients research-oriented questions, she knew that was not the type of interaction she should be having. Although her clients knew that she was also researching her practice, she recognized that it would be inappropriate to pursue her research at specific times in her work. Yet waiting for the right moment to raise the research the issues allows the actual point of practice to pass, and recollections about it can never be as vivid or as valid.

6. The practical knowledge recorded is subjective, as is the nature of knowledge itself; it is incomplete, but then few research reports can cover the whole of a practical or theoretical field; and its reliability cannot be validated apart from recognizing that what is recorded is as accurate as the subjects' memories. And of course, in self-reports it is always possible for people to misrepresent the facts for a variety of reasons, such as wishing to present themselves as more competent or more confident than they actually were in the situation. Readers of such records must always be aware of this possibility.

7. Action research seems anecdotal because traditional research seems a little more scientific. In the latter, the research conditions can be controlled, whereas those of practice for action research cannot be. In this sense, practice may not be scientific. But is this actually the case? Could it be that the controlled conditions of the scientific experiment are in fact more artificial than the uncontrolled conditions of practice? This form of action research reflects something of the actual reality of the practitioners, which the artificially controlled conditions of the "scientific" experiments fail to do. Genuine action research does not seek to control the conditions of the action, which is one of the reasons why it has not been accepted into the fold of scientific research. Both reflective practice and action research seek to understand, rather than control, the conditions in which the practice occurs. Indeed, any research into human practice that seeks to control the conditions is artificial, and it is wise to recognize the limitations of such research on human action. We should consequently be skeptical about the validity of some (but not all) "scientific" research into human behavior.

Thus this apparently obvious approach to research is fraught with difficulties, some of which may be insurmountable. Does this mean that practitioner-researchers are not reliable resources in researching their own practice? Clearly, they are the best source of a great deal of their own learning, reflecting, and acting, even if their written presentation of what they do might not be as well recorded as the research reports of a professional researcher. Indeed, the more traditional research methods cannot research a great deal of the personal and transitory facets of practice that action research can record about the nature of practice and the practitioner.

The conclusion is that whereas practitioner-researchers might be in a good position to record their practice, this might be best undertaken when they are either solving problems or posing problems; they may be a less reliable resource when they are merely engaged in recording routine skill performance. At the same time, certain aspects of the report's subjectivity have to be recognized, and other means of verifying it may be needed.

Participant Observation

The only form of traditional research that comes close to what I have described in this chapter is participative research, in which the researcher actually assumes an actor's role to explore the situation. In a sense, the researcher becomes a practitioner in order to understand the practice situation. In education and community work, there have been a number of studies (for example, Willis, 1977) in which the researcher assumes the role of a student or a member of a social group in order to "get inside" the situation and to record the experience as a participant. This overcomes some of the problems of the actors seeking to record their own situation. The observers learn to experience the practice situation in ways similar to how the practitioners themselves experience if, thereby enabling them to record a more accurate understanding of the experience. Bailey (1978) suggests four advantages of participant observation:

- Data collected can include nonverbal behavior.
- The observer is able to record information as it occurs.
- The observer is able to build up intimate and informal relationships with the subjects being researched.
- The observations are less reactive than other types of data-gathering methods.

These are among the advantages outlined in the discussion, and we will encounter them again in the next chapter, on collaborative research. Nevertheless, the participant still cannot record the feelings and emotions of the practitioners unless the relationships formed in the research process lead to cooperative approaches (Peters, 1997), which resemble but are not the same as collaborative research.

Conclusion

I began this chapter with the distinction between action orientation and research orientation because I consider that some practitioner-researchers' roles are already oriented toward recording, chronicling, and assessing. Other practitioner-researchers are concerned with the new practical knowledge, developed skills, and so on, for the sake of practice itself. Both are equally valid reasons for undertaking action research.

This chapter has also demonstrated that practitioner research has a great deal to commend it, because it captures something of the uniqueness of the practice itself. It cannot provide a perfect reflection of practice, but it gets closer than the more traditional research methods do. As this is recognized, the practitioner-researcher's role will assume a greater significance in late modern society. Even so, it might be possible for practitioner-researchers to be assisted in their research so that some of the problems noted in this chapter might be overcome. Collaborative research might enable practitioner-researchers to reflect even more precisely the practice processes in which they are engaged.

Chapter Nine

Collaborative Research

We saw in Chapter Eight that practitioner-researchers might not be able to research certain aspects of their practice, such as those that are tacit or habituated. Consequently, we have to look for other methods to help them probe these aspects of their role. Practitioner-researchers should still be involved as researchers, or all the advantages found in action research will be lost; collaborative approaches are the only ones that can enable practitioner-researchers to fulfill their research role while still experiencing practice itself.

Indeed, Torbert (1981a) makes the same claims for collaborative research that I have already made for action research: "The model of collaborative inquiry begins from the assumption that research and action, even though analytically distinguishable, are inextricably intertwined in practice. Knowledge is always gained through action and for action" (p. 145). Tom and Sork (1994) also highlight the difference in the type of knowledge gained by this approach when they claim that "findings that are the product of true collaborations between practitioners and academic researchers can and should be qualitatively different from the findings produced by either party working alone" (p. 54). They recognize the contribution that each can bring to the process.

Peters (1997) is clear that there is a difference between cooperation between practitioners and researchers and collaboration between them. It is suggested here that practitioner-researchers should collaborate with other researchers to achieve the most accurate interpretation of the practice event. For the purposes of this chapter, collaborative inquiry refers to collaboration between practitioner-researchers, between practitioner-researchers and practitioners, or between practitioner-researchers and researchers in precisely the way specified by Tom and Sork. Other forms of collaboration do occur, however, such as a team of researchers studying the same situation, comparative research in which researchers study more than one event, or collective case studies. Collaborative research, of the type being discussed here, can occur when the practitioner-researchers continue their practice while other practitioner-researchers or the researchers both observe that practice and then discuss it with the practitioners. In a sense, this is a triangulation of research methods made possible by the collaborative nature of the exercise. (See Cohen and Mannion, 1985, pp. 254–270, for a discussion of triangulation.)

Heron (1981, p. 157) has suggested that there are four stages in collaborative research:

1. The co-researchers discuss their initial research propositions and agree about working hypotheses.
2. The co-researchers, as joint subjects, apply these procedures and modify them accordingly.
3. The co-researchers become fully immersed in their mutual encounter and experience.
4. The co-researchers return to discuss their original research propositions and, taking account of their modifications, reach final conclusions.

For Heron, it is clear that it is not just the practice being researched that is discussed but the actual process of collaboration as well. Herein lies one of the potential problems with collaborative research: interpersonal dynamics can interfere with the process, and the findings might then be flawed. At the same time, it is the collaboration that is the fundamental strength of this approach, as I have suggested. Now we need to discuss this approach.

Conducting Collaborative Research

In a piece of collaborative action research into nursing care, Titchen (1996), a nurse researcher, collaborated with an expert nurse. She describes her strategy thus: "My research strategy, based on observing, listening, [and] questioning, . . . was designed to bring the phenomenon of patient-centered nursing as fully to consciousness as possible and to lay out its sense and ground" (p. 183). Not only did she observe, question, and consult papers, but she also presented research reports in collaboration with her expert nurse. Without the full and willing collaboration of the nurse, who was effectively a practitioner-researcher, Titchen would not have been able to bring to the attention of others the taken-for-granted elements of everyday nursing. She would certainly not have been able to show how patients and their relatives had completely misunderstood the intentions or the actions of the nurse in the example cited in Chapter Three or how the expert nurse sought to diffuse their misinterpretations without causing offense.

In a sense we can discern four elements in this research:

- Observing and recording the practice
- Seeking to understand how the practitioner-researcher thought and felt about the practice
- Seeking to see if the researcher's interpretations are valid
- Demonstrating something of the dialectical relationship between knowledge, beliefs, feelings, and so on, and the practice situation

I briefly discuss each of these in turn.

Observing and Recording Practice

Researchers are able to be present in the practice situation and record the ongoing process. This can be undertaken most unobtrusively by the researchers' taking notes as the process unfolds. It would also be possible, however, to record the events on a tape recorder or on video. The more obvious the recording, however, the more likely it is to artificialize the situation.

At the same time, it is possible for the practitioners to speak into a microphone as the process happens, recording something of their innermost feelings, the way they are reasoning about practice, and so on. This provides an additional record of the events.

Understanding the Practitioner's Perspective

Having observed practice, researchers know something about what actually happened in terms of doing. If there is a practitioner record of the events, something about the practitioner's perspective already exists. It is then possible, on the basis of these records, to discuss with practitioners their intentions and their process knowledge. Only through dialogue can the practitioners' practical reasoning be reliably revealed and recorded. This is also possible by videotaping practice and then discussing the recording to bring to conscious awareness some of the practitioners' tacit knowledge, taken-for-grantedness of practice, reasoning, feelings, and so on.

Herein lie the skills of the researcher, as an expert interviewer with all the sensitivities of being able to unravel the complex process of human behavior through personal interaction.

Checking the Researcher's Interpretations

These interviews are not interrogative: they are part of a cooperative process in which the researchers' own interpretations of the events are discussed with the practitioners. It is in this aspect of the process that some of the tacit assumptions of the practitioners might be brought to light and, at the same time, some of the assumptions, misinformation, and biases of the researchers (something we all have about most situations) can be corrected.

One of my master's degree students, a nurse educator, spent time working with student nurses, watching them practice and then interviewing them afterward about their own understanding of their practice. In this way, she was able to understand more clearly what she had seen, and also to check her own interpretations of what she observed. This is cooperative research, although it is not hard to see that similar research processes could be totally collaborative.

Demonstrating the Practitioner's Theory-Practice Relationship

In this process, the dialogical relationship between thought, feelings, and action may be seen and discussed. By knowing how the practitioners related the role performance and their knowledge, feelings, and so on, it is possible to see how they relate their own theory with their practice.

Finally, a report is drawn up, all the collaborators review it to make it as accurate as possible, and the final version is published.

Discussion

Within this collaborative framework of research, some of the problems mentioned earlier can be overcome, yield benefits such as these:

- The practitioners can more efficiently perform their practice role while still engaging in a research role.
- The effects of practitioners' tacit knowledge or habituation can be revealed in the role performance and discussed with the collaborators.
- Discussing beliefs, values, and inner emotions with their collaborators provides a more complete picture of the behavior being researched.
- The practitioners' practical reasoning can be uncovered and recorded.
- The practitioner-researchers need not have a full repertoire of research skills because the collaborators are skilled researchers.

- The collaborators can also interpret how the performers present themselves and help them overcome individual political problems.
- Gaps in the practitioners' memory can be filled in.
- The research will not be regarded as either anecdotal or as a mere repetition of similar reports elsewhere.

Moreover, some of the hermeneutic problems of observational research can also be overcome, since the researchers can discuss their interpretations of the behavior they observe with the practitioners themselves and modify the interpretations accordingly (Heron, 1981; Carr and Kemmis, 1985).

Through dialogue and collaboration, this form of research not only overcomes many of the problems with practitioner-researchers in action research but also many of the problems of the more traditional research paradigm. It can reveal the inner subjective experiences of the practitioners as well as their external behaviors. It does not, however, resolve all the problems of researching practice. For instance, the findings reported still only record the specific event, and future reflective practice by the same practitioner may well not support the findings of the published collaborative research project. Consequently, the validity of the findings is always restricted to the events recorded and cannot be legitimately generalized. At the same time, because this is a form of triangulation, the collaboration itself is an additional factor in the internal validity of the research itself. It is both a major strength and a potential weakness.

Collaboration demands a sense of mutual respect, trust, and support, a democratic enterprise in which all collaborators respect the skills of their counterparts. Torbert (1981b) found these difficult to gain in his own piece of collaborative inquiry; he reports that he "had not anticipated how unconvincing he would be, and how little interest and how much resistance others would manifest, about the ideal of collaborative inquiry" (p. 440). One reason for resistance is that individuals do not actually see this small-scale qualitative research as genuine research because they have the quantitative paradigm in mind.

The practitioners should be expert practitioners, and the researchers should be expert researchers. It is clear, however, that the research skills required in this form of research are a little different from those required in traditional research. Reinharz (1981) points out that research collaborators require all the skills of the old research paradigm, plus skills in interpersonal relations, counseling and interviewing, and self-awareness, and a supportive approach to each other.

There is a danger, I have found, with researchers who have counseling and interpersonal skills: they may fail to draw boundaries. One of my own research students, an experienced counselor, using these techniques, explained to me how difficult she found it to avoid playing her counseling role with some of the people with whom she was collaborating in her research.

Practitioner-researchers can only conduct research that is case-specific, whether it is done individually or in collaboration, so their findings can be regarded only as pertaining to the particular situation. Three important points emerge from this discussion.

First, the findings they report can be treated as relevant only to the time and place when the research was conducted. The practitioners' practical knowledge will continue to evolve as a result of the changes in the practice situation from which they continue to learn.

Second, the reported findings reflect the practical knowledge of the practitioners but do not constitute knowledge for the readers of the research; they merely provide information about a specific situation. Knowledge is always subjective, and information is only potential knowledge for its recipients.

Third, case studies are inductive; that is, particular information can lead to specific conclusions. Because one case study would not provide sufficient information to allow generalizations to be drawn, Stake (1994) proposed collective case studies that would provide more data from which generalizations might be drawn. Such an approach naturally raises some of the problems of more traditional quantitative research: the nature of the collection, or sample, would then need to be discussed; once data were gathered, researchers would need to have criteria for selecting the information from the different case studies; and so on. Once embarked on, however, the process of generalization becomes one of distillation, and detailed information, often specific to one case, becomes lost in the final generalized conclusions. Seeking to generalize is to remove the conclusions yet another step away from the realities of practice and consequently to information that may be no more than a subjective interpretation of a generalized representation of the reality of practice.

Conclusion

Collaborative methods seem to overcome many of the problems of the practitioners' serving as their own researchers. Records can be compiled and published that get as close to the facts of a unique event as possible. Indeed, practitioner-researchers can overcome many of the problems with action research with this approach, although the findings are still a representation of the reality they purport to record.

Practitioner-researchers are occasionally required to conduct research of a more traditional nature. The final two chapters of Part Three examine documentary research and small-scale surveys.

Chapter Ten

Using Documents

Practitioner-researchers are rather like ethnographic researchers, because a great deal of their research deals with nondocumentary sources. Indeed, the study of practice as it occurs can be purely ethnographic, but like ethnographers, practitioner-researchers do have the opportunity of using documents both to help understand practice and, even more, to understand the situation within which practice occurs. There is, according to Hammersley and Atkinson (1983), "a quite bewildering variety of documentary materials that might be of some relevance to the researcher. These might be arranged along a dimension from the most 'informal' to the 'formal' or 'official'" (p. 129). Among the documents that are available to practitioner-researchers are practitioners' notes, case notes, minutes of meetings, policy and procedure documents, and other published research on similar areas of study.

This chapter therefore starts by looking at the types of document that can assist in understanding practice itself; it then examines the documentary material that can help us understand the situation within which practice occurs; the third section looks at the more traditional published literature; and the final section makes some suggestions about how practitioner-researchers might use the documents, allowing for the fact that most of these have been constructed for specific purposes and must be approached accordingly. It must be noted from the outset, however, that such material does not tell us anything about the actual process of practice, although it can enrich our understanding of it in a variety of ways.

Documents About Practice

Practitioners, practitioner-researchers, and new interns frequently keep diaries about their practice, often quite informal ones. This is especially true of interns who are expected by their professors to keep full records of their learning in diaries, learning logs, reflective journals, or other documents. Practitioners themselves frequently make notes of events in their practice, often rough notes as an aide-mémoire about an event. Professors often keep full notes on their graduate students' research progress.

In addition, there are more formal reports made about practice: schoolteachers write reports on the children in their class for parents; community workers, nurses, and doctors make case notes about their clients and patients; and so on. Indeed, the introduction of the computer has probably resulted in more records about practice being kept than ever before.

All of this material might prove useful for practitioner-researchers who seek to understand practice more thoroughly—if they can gain access to it. Thus arise various ethical considerations about the use of some documentary material.

Indeed, practitioner-researchers can keep, and ask their colleagues to write, journals about their practice as part of the research process. They can even provide quite specific guidance about the types of things they would like recorded. The more specific the guidance, however, the more likely it is that practitioner-researchers will get what they are looking for rather than what the practitioners themselves considered important for them to record.

Naturally, getting material that practitioners and practitioner-researchers themselves have prepared about their own practice means that practitioner-researchers can get closer to understanding the practice process itself. Diaries and notes about specific events are clearly very useful, although it must be recognized once again that practitioners probably make many more notes about critical incidents in their practice than they do about the habitual and tacit aspects of their work. In a study of health visitors (nurse social workers) in the United Kingdom, Dingwall (1977) showed that ordinarily only unusual events were recorded.

Many practitioners are expected to keep case notes about their work, especially about students, patients, and clients. These notes are often prepared so that supervisors or managers can see them. Indeed, such "formal" notes allow managers to exercise control over practitioners, so although the notes can be useful and informative, practitioner-researchers must never lose sight of the fact that they have been prepared for a specific purpose. Practitioners prepare these notes with the ultimate purpose in mind, not as literal accounts of what occurred in practice. Like anyone writing for an audience, practitioners who know that someone is going to read their notes will write them with that specific audience and its purpose for reading in mind. Consequently, studying such documents requires active deconstruction of what is recorded.

If, therefore, practitioner-researchers want to understand the reasoning behind specific events, it is important that they try to interview the writers of the documents after having read them. In this way, it is possible to begin to probe the reasoning process of the practitioners, which might reveal more about the practice itself and even help the practitioners become more consciously aware of the actual practice process than they were when they wrote the report. Such documents, therefore, are useful accessories to understanding the practice because they capture a view of this transitory process and shed some light both on what occurred and on the reasoning and feelings of the practitioners.

Documents About the Practice Situation

More formal documents exist about most practices, such as minutes of meetings, official correspondence, policy directives, outlines of procedures, statements from management, rule books, job descriptions, and so on. Many of these documents are in the public domain and can be accessed by any interested party. Many others, however, are relatively confidential so that practitioner-researchers wishing to use them for research purposes might need to obtain permission from the issuing authority.

Some of these documents prescribe procedures that might be designed to protect practitioners in the event of litigation, but almost incidentally they also inhibit experimentation and innovation. Such documents lessen the art and transitory nature of practice by trying to introduce some conformity into it, a conformity that might be at the level of appearance rather than practitioner experience. For instance, conforming individuals might be perfectly happy with elaborate procedures and rule books about practice, whereas more independent types might find their job satisfaction decreasing with each additional prescribed procedure. Practitioner-researchers are perhaps well placed to study job satisfaction among their colleagues because they are aware of such inhibiting but protective measures.

These more formal documents might lay down certain parameters for practice. Minutes of meetings might record the reasons that management teams reach the decisions they do about practice, official correspondence might reveal the constraints placed on management, and so forth.

These documents are more generally applicable to all practitioners, so they do not in themselves tell us about practice. Nevertheless, they describe generalized conditions that have to be taken into account in seeking to understand the particulars of any practice process.

Once again, however, documents of this nature should never be taken at face value. Each document has been drafted for a specific purpose. Meeting minutes, for example, are usually very carefully constructed. Not only what they contain but also what they omit is important. For example, a few weeks before I wrote this chapter I participated in a business meeting at which one of the points raised was potentially embarrassing to the company organizing the meeting. Significantly, the company representative omitted the item from the minutes and organized the next meeting informally over lunch so that there was no opportunity for the omission to be discussed. Clearly it is essential to understand the purposes underlying a document and to recognize that documents about practice should not be swallowed whole if the procedures surrounding practice are to be thoroughly understood. Indeed, Hammersley and Atkinson (1983) support this contention: "Official documents and statistics should be treated as social products; they must be *examined,* not simply used as a resource. To treat them as a resource and not a topic is to trade on the interpretive and interactional work that went into their production, to treat as a reflection or document of the world phenomena that are actually produced by it" (p. 137).

This can become a problem for practitioner-researchers because so much of the outcomes of their research is open to management to read. If management's spin on official documents is exposed and deconstructed, management might not treat the practitioner-researchers with sympathy and might seek to curtail their research. Once again, the political nature of the research process becomes quite apparent.

Formal Literature Searches

"For most topics," suggest Merriam and Simpson (1995, p. 34), "there are two kinds of literature: the theoretical or the conceptual writing in the area and data-based research studies." They go on to suggest that the library reference room is the place to begin the literature search. Of course, they are partly right for the traditional type of research, although autobiography and biography and other forms of literature might also be useful in many projects. But as we have seen, practitioner-researchers undertake a different form of research, and they might seek to use some "insider" documents that might never find their way into the library or the reference room. Nevertheless, the more traditional approaches to literature search still constitute a part of the practitioner-researchers' projects. Researchers do need to be aware of the published literature on their topics, just as they must recognize its limitations.

The functions of the traditional literature search, according to Merriam and Simpson (1995, pp. 32–33) are to provide a foundation for building knowledge; show how a study advances, refines, or revises what is already known; help conceptualize the study; provide clues to methodology and instrumentation; and offer a collective point of reference for interpreting the researcher's own findings.

Obviously, relevant literature might help clarify the practitioner-researchers' own thinking about aspects of their research project. There is a danger, however, with a great deal of practitioner research—and even with traditional research work—that the knowledge sought from the literature about the topic is limited specifically to that subject. For example, researchers wanting to understand the teaching process might restrict their reading to research literature about teaching and fail to read the literature on power, ethics, personal relationships, and other relevant areas, all of which may provide different perspectives on the same process. Consequently, the way in which researchers interpret their data can be restricted by the breadth or narrowness of their reading.

Theoretically, literature searches are undertaken at the outset of a study, and in this way, Merriam and Simpson can claim that the literature search helps provide clues about methodology and instrumentation. This might only be partly correct because, as I have suggested already, a great deal of practitioner research is iterative. Reading the literature continues simultaneously with the research project, creating an interactive process between the knowledge gained from reading and that gained from undertaking the research in a practice situation. The literature might therefore provide clues about the ongoing direction of the project; it might reinforce the types of insight that practitioner-researchers are gaining or make them reconsider their initial understandings; or it might provide alternative ways of interpreting the data.

Once again, however, it is wise to treat the literature as a social construction—a "field of cultural production" (Bourdieu, 1993)—and study it accordingly. Let us explore this process of interpretation to understand more thoroughly what lies behind the words on the written page.

Interpreting the Written Word

Potter (1996) has a nice metaphor to describe what happens in the process of representing reality through words: he suggests that there is a mirror and a construction yard. Language is like a mirror, reflecting how things are, but the mirror might actually be blurred so that it distorts reality. In contrast, descriptions construct the world inasmuch as we learn to see the world through the descriptions we have and perhaps interpret it accordingly, but they are also constructions of how others want us to see the world.

"Authors will have interests in presenting themselves in a (usually) favourable light; they may have axes to grind, scores to settle, or excuses or justifications to make. They are often written with the benefit of hindsight, and are thus subject to the usual problems of long-term recall. Authors have a sense of audience that will lead them to put particular glosses on their accounts" (Hammersley and Atkinson, 1983, p. 130). These are the biases that Gadamer (1976) claims to be the "prejudices [that] constitute our being" (p. 9). It is for this reason that we have to reflect on what we read and see the prejudices that help construct the written word; then we are in a position to reach behind what we see and get a step closer to the reality that the words purport to represent.

We do not, however, actually reach that reality. Indeed, there might not actually be a reality to reach. For instance, consider a description of a practice event, enshrined in the written word: practitioner-researchers might deconstruct the description and reach beyond it—but to what? Practice is transitory and ephemeral. There is no empirical reality underlying the description against which to assess the report. Consequently, deconstruction and reinterpretation still amount only to another interpretation. In seeking to understand practice, practitioner-researchers are always dealing with the transitory and with representations of reality. Indeed, in dealing with any document, we must always recognize that it is a representation, and though it might "mirror" reality, it is itself a construction.

Consequently, practitioner-researchers must always recognize that documents might only throw light of varying intensities on the processes they are researching. Some of the documents, for instance, will provide reasons that their original recipients have acted as they have—that they have prescribed practice or, in other words, constructed a reality. At the same time, they are themselves constructions. They are phenomena that have to be treated as part of the research process, rather than as empirical data for it.

Conclusion

Practitioner-researchers have potential access to a wide variety of documentary material, much of which is "insider" information. This places certain constraints on its use and raises significant ethical and political considerations but enriches the research process. This documentary evidence provides greater insights into practice and practice situations. But the documents have to be treated as part of their research process to be interpreted and understood at the appropriate level rather than as factual records of evidence.

Practitioner-researchers also use formally published material that finds its way into libraries and resource centers. They have to use this material in precisely the same way as other researchers would in traditional research projects. But then practitioner-researchers do actually undertake small-scale survey-type research projects about their practice situations in a more traditional manner. The next chapter examines the small-scale survey research project.

Chapter Eleven

Small-Scale Surveys

Both action and collaborative action research, as they have been described in the preceding chapters, are reflective processes. They involve practitioners and practitioner-researchers in action and reflection, in rather the same way as Freire (1972) described praxis. The research and the practice are interrelated.

In Chapter Ten, however, we recognized that practitioner-researchers are also in a position to examine documents in their research, often "insider" documents. Such examination constitutes research about practice rather than research into practice itself. Practitioner-researchers also use small-scale quantitative research in some of their projects. In these projects, they tend to look at the practitioners, at their attitudes toward practice, and at the situation in which the practice is conducted. Practice is treated in a more objectified manner, more like a fact than a transitory process.

Practitioner-researchers tend to use the traditional quantitative methods, such as questionnaires and interview, in these research projects. Although this chapter is not intended as a how-to chapter, it examines the types of topics that might be researched in this way. Recently, for instance, a practitioner-researcher who taught reflective practice at the local university school of nursing and midwifery wanted to discover how nurses and midwives used reflective practice in their own work, so she attempted to design a questionnaire that would allow her to do so. She used her questionnaire in a small-scale sample survey of approximately one hundred practitioners in the hospital. The exercise involved reading about reflective practice, sampling theory, questionnaire design, statistical analysis of data, and an evaluation of her research project. Even so, the responses she obtained were the practitioners' own interpretations of reflective practice and what they wanted her, a teacher of the subject, to know about what they actually did.

This chapter is divided into six brief sections: the validity of subjects chosen for quantitative research, sampling theory, interview and questionnaire design, the research process, analysis of data, and evaluation of the research process.

Validity of the Research Question

Many years ago, when I taught and researched in the field of sociology of religion, I presented a theoretical paper at an international conference. At the end of the presentation, a member of the audience, a well-known sociologist, said to me that he thought the paper was very interesting but he wondered whether I had an unresearchable topic. At the time I was not sure what he meant, but now I feel I know. There are certain topics that cannot legitimately be researched by traditional methods, which is certainly true in this book. For instance, we cannot discover any "facts" about the practice process through the use of a questionnaire to one hundred practitioners because practice itself is not a "fact." All we might be able to discover is what practitioners think at the time of the research about specific aspects of their practice.

In a sense, this section involves us in a brief excursion into the philosophy of social research (see, for example, Williams and May, 1996). I have already implied that practice itself is transitory and ephemeral, so it is not ever a researchable fact in the empirical sense. Consequently, methods that try to research facts are not valid research tools in seeking to understand the uniqueness of the practice process. In action research, however, the practitioner-researchers are involved in the practice and both create it and interpret it. In their accounts, they try to record accurately, and interpret, what is going on during the process. Moreover, once they have recorded it, the record becomes historical because it can never occur again in precisely the same way.

In survey-type research, the practitioner-researchers stand outside the phenomena they are researching and seek to understand them, but those phenomena are still not empirical facts. Practitioner-researchers can seek to understand the constructions of meaning that others place on their practice, their reactions to that practice, and so forth. These meanings are factual, without necessarily being facts, but they relate only to the time when the research is undertaken because attitudes, knowledge, and many other things change.

We also have to recognize that because these accounts are constructions, they are neither empirical nor value-free. No matter how objective practitioner-researchers try to be, they are studying human beings who have values, attitudes, and so on, and who construct their responses to any form of research tool. Even sophisticated designs that try to overcome some of the respondents' psychological predispositions in response to questionnaires do so only to a limited degree. Even then, the practitioner-researchers' own interpretation of the data is itself influenced by their own constructions of the world, which means that they are actively constructing interpretations rather than providing totally objective explanations of facts. The results of such research are representations of reality rather than true reflections of it, no matter how rigorous the research methodology happens to be. The fact, however, that the outcomes of such research are still representations is no excuse for not being rigorous in research design. Poorly designed research produces even more inaccurate representations of reality than well-designed research instruments; that is why the remainder of this chapter concentrates on this issue.

Sampling Theory

Although we cannot delve into the intricacies of research methodology here, it is necessary to recognize that any sample will only approximate the entire population when the sample is taken, that some types of sample are regarded as more accurate than others, and that different types of samples tell us different things about the practice situation. Indeed, the sample is based on a probability that it will enable the researcher to understand the social world. If the sample is sufficiently large and accurate, we can estimate the degree of probability that the results will reflect the reality that the research is seeking to reveal. The case study, you will recall, is such a small sample that it is very problematic to try to generalize from such a study.

Practitioner-researchers are rarely in a position to research the whole of a profession or to conduct a national sample, so their sampling frames are more restricted: schoolteacher practitioner-researchers might seek to research teachers in their school or their district; nurses and doctors to research practice situations in their own hospital; management consultants to understand consultancy situations in their own company; and so on. A small sampling frame like this one, however, actually constitutes a whole population if the research question relates only to a specific location of practice, such as a university or a company, and this might actually be the case if the research is being conducted to answer a management or local policy question. Consequently, as long as the research question is specifically framed within a restricted context, the research is much more manageable for practitioner-researchers.

Cohen and Mannion (1985, pp. 98–101) suggest that there are ten different types of samples, and practitioner-researchers should be aware of the approach they are employing, and of its strengths and weaknesses.

1. *Simple random.* A random sample is selected from the total population in such a way that every member of the population has an equal chance of being selected. The problem with all randomized approaches, however, is that the total population is often not depicted anywhere. In my own doctoral research into the members of a profession, one organization's records were nearly two years out of date, so determining an accurate sampling frame was nearly impossible for that professional group. For practitioner-researchers, the population might be the number of practitioners in their company or district rather than the national population of practitioners.

2. *Systematic random sample*. An accurate sampling frame is constructed, and the cases to be studied are selected systematically—for example, every tenth case on the list, with the first one being randomly drawn from the first ten.

3. *Stratified random sample*. The population is subdivided into categories and then a random sample is taken from each category.

4. *Cluster sample*. To study an aspect of the practice of, say, teaching medicine, it might be convenient to select randomly a number of medical schools in a given location and then study the aspect of practice chosen for each teacher in those schools.

5. *Stage sample*. It might not be convenient to study each teacher in the cluster chosen, so a second random sample or the teachers in each cluster might then be approached.

6. *Convenience sample*. Researchers select a random sample from a convenient population.

7. *Quota sample*. The researcher selects a specified proportion of each category the researcher seeks to study.

8. *Purposive sample*. The researcher hand-picks the subject to be studied so that, for instance, expert teachers, as defined by their colleagues, in a college or university might be studied to see what common characteristics they have.

9. *Dimensional sample*. This is a type of quota sample in which researchers not only select the quota to be studied but also ensure that all the dimensions of the practice to be studied are included in the sample.

10. *Snowball sample*. This might begin with the small number of experts who were identified by their peers, who in turn identify others whom they regard as experts, so the sample grows.

The type of sample taken for research depends to a great extent on the purpose of the research. If the research is seeking a broad picture of the whole population, random sampling of the population should be used, but if it is seeking a small population for in-depth research, the snowballing, purposive, quota, or cluster approach might be more useful. Obviously, for practitioner-researchers, convenience forms a major criterion in the way they select their approach to their project, although many of the samples described here can be used in small-scale research.

Instrument Design

There is a temptation for busy practitioner-researchers to seek to use a predesigned research instrument for their research, because they feel that it both adds validity to their research and saves time. Regardless of how attractive this approach might seem to be, it is often misplaced, because the predesigned research instrument has not always been prepared in response to the practitioner-researchers' own research questions—unless the research is a replication of a previous study. Naturally such instruments can be adapted and might prove useful, but it is frequently more accurate to design an instrument specifically for the individual project.

In contrast, another temptation of the small-scale research project is to prepare a new research instrument in a rather hasty manner. Such an approach will result in even greater inaccuracy in the representation of the reality being researched. More haste does not necessarily mean greater speed. A former colleague of mine came to see me about designing a questionnaire for some research he was undertaking—to begin in the next two or three days. He assumed that questionnaire design is a simple undertaking. But if practitioner-researchers are to discover data that in any way approximate reality, their questionnaire design or interview schedules need to be very carefully considered and tested before they are used. Small scale is no excuse for a lack of rigor.

Consequently, practitioner-researchers should endeavor to use the most rigorous approaches in design and testing their instrument, even though this might be a time-consuming process. This is also true of the letter attached to the questionnaire or whatever initial approach is made to the potential respondents. Such care will almost certainly improve the response rate. I know a number of social scientists who will not respond to poorly designed research instruments on the grounds that if the researchers cannot be bothered to design them well, the scientists cannot be bothered to answer them. Nevertheless, the fact that the researchers are also practitioners needs to be stressed in this initial approach, because practitioner-researchers are insiders to the practice situation, and this might engender a more sympathetic orientation toward the research from the potential respondents.

The Research Process

Practitioner-researchers, conducting survey-type research, need to recognize that this form of research takes a considerable amount of time and effort. Research is a complex and ethical process; undertaking it requires the ability to work alone on occasion and to cope with the emotional and mental pressures of pursuing the work.

Testing the instrument, the letter of introduction, and other materials takes time. Constructing a sampling frame and selecting a sample is not necessarily easy, although many sampling frames already exist, such as the number of employees in an organization. I have already discussed sampling, but I have not really focused on interviewing. This is a skillful process, and it is wise for practitioner-researchers who are going to undertake interview research to have some awareness of the pitfalls. Individuals who have not been trained in interviewing might be well advised to take a brief course. Just as there are different types of samples, so there are different types of interviews. They may be face to face or at a distance (telephone); they may take place at a location chosen by the researcher, by the interviewee, or by mutual agreement; they may be tightly structured or open-ended; they may involve different forms of questioning; they may use prompts, such as photographs, to stimulate discussion; they may be one-on-one or in a group; they may involve advanced warning of the topics for discussion or no forewarning; they may be recorded in different way (written notes, audio, or video); and they may be followed up in a variety of ways (Blaxter, Hughes, and Tight, 1996).

Interviews are also time-consuming, and practitioner-researchers may choose to undertake only a few. If they are tape-recorded, for instance, it can take ten or more hours (Blaxter, Hughes, and Tight, 1996, report seventeen hours) to transcribe and contextualize every one-hour taped interview. The types of interviews chosen will depend on the research questions and the ways that the practitioner-researchers can get their subjects to respond to the topics under review.

Frequently, practitioner-researchers will use more than one method in seeking to answer their research question, such as a few in-depth interviews followed by a questionnaire survey, or vice versa. This approach is referred to as multistage research. It is also a form of triangulation, which is simply using more than one approach to focus on the same phenomenon in order to get a more accurate picture—even though, in this case, the picture will still be only a representation.

Data Analysis

Small-scale surveys still yield statistical data and should not be conducted by individuals who have no knowledge of statistics. Some practitioner-researchers figure that all they need to do is record the numbers of respondents who answer each question in one way or another. They are wrong. Quantitative data require sophisticated analyses; it is important for practitioner-researchers to have some awareness of statistical techniques before they undertake any quantitative research project. Statistical analyses need to be conducted on all statistical data, within the limitations of the design of the research.

We have already noted that data, which might give the impression of being empirical, are constructions of the respondents' reality and also reflect their reasons for participating in the study in the first place. These reasons might well relate to the way the practitioner-researchers presented the research project, so the data must always be analyzed with these points in mind.

In addition, empirical data, such as numbers, have no intrinsic meaning. For instance, the fact that ten respondents agreed with a proposition that "practicing with an organization seeking to be a learning organization is more interesting than practicing in a bureaucratic one" is not a very meaningful finding in itself. The data become meaningful only when they are interpreted. Thus the idea of "analyzing" data perhaps conveys a false impression, because what is occurring is a process of interpreting them. Practitioner-researchers are consequently more likely to have different orientations to their interpretation than researchers who are outsiders to the practice.

The presentation of data analyses must therefore always recognize the processes in the construction of the information contained therein, relating to a specific group of respondents who replied at a given time. Their responses are social constructions, and so are the researchers' interpretations of those responses. Sweeping claims for the research should never be made—the research does not allow for it—but it is essential to try to assess the validity of the findings.

Assessing the Validity of the Research

Practitioner-researcher research usually begins with a question about practice, rather than a question about theoretical interpretations of practice. Sometimes the question is prompted by curiosity or interest; other times it might stem from a management requirement; and so on. The question needs to be answered, although there are certain limitations to every research process, as has become clear from this chapter.

The question is answered by respondents when the research takes place. Do the research findings of small research projects have any wider validity? The answers to the research question might provide hypotheses about the wider field of practice, hypotheses for future research projects on a wider scale, or even for other small-scale projects, but they do not actually provide any certainty about the field—even when the research was conducted—nor do they allow management or anyone else to predict with certainty based on the findings. I noted when we looked at sampling theory that sampling is based on probability. We can only conclude that the degree of probability that this form of research can capture about some aspects of social reality is limited, but the more focused, rigorous, and specific the research is, the greater is the likelihood that the results will provide a tenable hypothesis about the phenomenon under investigation.

Finally, practitioner-researchers do need to reflect on any small-scale survey that they have undertaken and discuss the validity of both their research methods and the findings. The clarity of the representation of reality presented is always dependent on the research methods and how they are used, so practitioner-researchers must be aware of the strengths and limitations of all aspects of their research undertaking.

Conclusion

Practitioner-researchers can conduct small-scale research surveys, but, by these methods, they cannot actually research practice itself, although they can research practitioners' attitudes toward practice and even toward aspects of their own espoused theory about practice and so on. Such surveys can also reveal attitudes toward management and policy formulations. They do have a degree of validity. Small-scale survey research thus has a role in the practitioner-researchers' research repertoire, although its focus is on the practitioners and the situation of practice rather than on the process of practice itself.

The chapters in Part Three have examined relevant aspects of practitioner-researchers' research orientation and have reached a number of conclusions that reflect on our understanding of practice, on our knowledge of practice, and on the practitioners' knowledge of practice. Part Four brings this discussion together and reaches a number of conclusions about the nature of theory and the relationship between practice and theory before we move on, in Part Five, to examine some of the implications of our discussion about practitioner-researchers in a wider social context.

Part Four

Practice and Theory

Chapter Twelve

Developing a Personal Theory

The main themes that have run through this book to this point refer to the fact that the practitioner-researcher has a dual role: as practitioner and researcher. Part Four serves as a linchpin that holds the whole together. It both reflects on what has gone before and lays the groundwork for what follows in Part Five.

The chapter has two main sections, reflecting our dual concerns: the practitioner's practice and the practitioner-researcher's practice of research.

The Practitioner's Practice

Earlier in this book we noted that practice is ever changing in this rapidly changing world; practice is both ephemeral and transitory. This means that in every practice situation, practitioners can presume on their practice for a only minimal period of time before it will change and new knowledge and skills will have to be learned. We have suggested that practitioners' practical knowledge is always changing in response to the changes that are occurring. Indeed, the French social philosopher Jean-François Lyotard (1984) has suggested that knowledge is rather like a narrative that is always describing what is and responding to the changing situations, and that it can be regarded as legitimate only when it can be performed. In this sense, then, practice is an art form, since practitioners are always adapting their practice to suit changing conditions.

Schön (1983) rightly recognized practice to be an art, and Argyris and Schön ([1974] 1992) noted that practitioners seem to have two forms of theory: espoused theory and theory in use. They tend to suggest that these two forms of theory are rather static, although there is naturally the implication that the theory in use is an adaptation of espoused theory as a result of the experiences of practice. I am suggesting here, however, that practitioners' practical knowledge is always undergoing change as they adapt their practice to the changing circumstances and learn, almost incidentally, from what they innovate in response to these changed conditions.

Practice is not the only source of change, however; practitioners are exposed to a variety of new information from other sources, such as professional journals, other practitioners, and continuing education. They are also exposed to work that has been undertaken in other academic disciplines about their fields of practice. This I want to call metatheory—a concept to which we will return in Chapter Thirteen. Practitioners might endeavor to incorporate some of these new ideas, this metatheory, into their own practice and test them out.

Further, there are various dimensions of practitioners' theories about practice and their actual knowledge about what works for them. For instance, they may have ideals about their profession that they wish they could put into practice but do not because they do not consider them sufficiently practical, realistic, or acceptable to their organization or profession.

Nevertheless, we can see that a practitioner's theory of practice is always subject to change—it is dynamic. Moreover, the theory is individual and subjective, since it is the individual practitioner who has innovated in a uniquely changing practice situation and learned from the experiences.

This uniqueness does not make one practitioner's theory entirely different from that of other practitioners in the same field; indeed, it cannot be. Practitioners have received similar preparation; they are subject to the same rules, regulations, and procedures of practice; they are exposed to the same professional journals and continuing education courses; and they share many other influences. Consequently, they have a similar habitus. But they do not all respond to the pressures to change in the same manner.

There are therefore both similarities and differences regarding practice, practice situations, and theories of practice in any given field; this we would expect. In the past, the tendency has been to emphasize the similarities rather than the differences, but that has not accurately reflected reality. Nevertheless, we can claim with confidence that practice and practical knowledge are *individual, personal, subjective,* and *dynamic*.

We have also made the point that practical knowledge is integrated rather than subdivided by academic discipline. At the same time, there are similarities among different practices, among different practitioners' understanding of their practice, and among their different theories of practice.

Practitioners' practical knowledge is dynamic because they continue to learn in their work situation, and we can perhaps depict this process most clearly as shown in Figure 12.1. In the figure there is a loop that incorporates a number of stages; the practitioners

1. Enter a work situation (practice situation 1) and practice

2. Reflect on the practice

3. Incorporate into their reflection any professional updating or reading they have undertaken—that is, any metatheory to which they have been exposed

4. Learn and develop their own personal theory, which they test in practice situation 2

The loop is then repeated continuously in practice.

It is significant that Figure 12.1 also embodies Freire's (1972) discussion about praxis, in which he writes, "The act of knowing involves a dialectical movement which goes from action to reflection and from reflection upon action to new action" (p. 31).

The point is that professionals' way of knowing is a dialectical movement from action to reflection, in a continuing loop. It is a

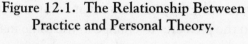

**Figure 12.1. The Relationship Between
Practice and Personal Theory.**

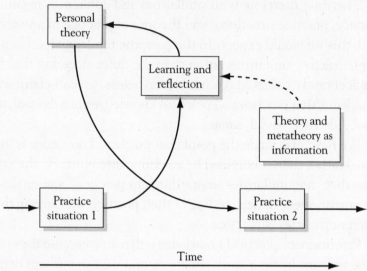

process of knowing, and what the practitioners have learned is their own knowledge.

The relationship between practical knowledge and practice is pragmatic. As Heller (1984) writes, "The pragmatic relationship denotes a direct unity of theory and practice" (p. 166). In other words, there is no disjuncture between the practitioners' theory and practice, which reads rather differently from the idea that has prevailed for many years concerning the problem of the relationship between theory and practice—a point to which we shall return in the next two chapters.

If there is a gap between the practitioners' theory and practice (disjuncture), however, then the practitioners are in a learning situation from which they have to adjust their practice and learn from their innovations. It is in this uniqueness of practice, where practitioners are adjusting and innovating, often with considerable rapidity, that practice becomes an art form.

Even so, it is the ability to problematize the taken for granted and the ability to impose ideals about imperfect situations and endeavor to change them that result in practitioners' improving their practice and moving upward along the pathway toward expertise. It is reflective learning (Jarvis, 1992), or double-loop learning (Argyris and Schön, [1974] 1992)—basically the same concept— that leads to improved performance and new knowledge about practice.

The Practitioner-Researcher's Research

Practitioner-researchers attempt to research practice and practical knowledge and report on the aspects they have researched. We have explored some of the strengths and limitations of research into practice and practical knowledge. We have acknowledged that in-depth studies into the unique and transitory—for example, case studies, action research, and collaborative research—allow us to get close to aspects of the ephemeral process, whereas more quantitative research methods enable us to see different dimensions of the situatedness of practice from a distance. Thus quantitative studies do reveal something of the similarities and differences between different practitioners and their situations.

Once practitioner-researchers report on their practice, however, there are similarities in the nature of the reports that did not exist in the different approaches to research. Significantly, these are similar to other research reports that are not conducted by practitioner-researchers, even though it is claimed here that they get closer to the realities they report than outside researchers do. The following are just some of the things they have in common:

- The reports are representations of reality.
- What they report is a social construct.
- The reports are distillations from the complexity of the practice situation, rather than documents incorporating

and embodying the whole—that is, they are always simplifications.

- The reports are bounded by time, so they necessarily reflect the past rather than the present.
- The reports contain the researchers' knowledge of what they report—but that knowledge is merely information for those who read it, until they learn it.
- The mediated information has to be tested by the recipients before they can accept its validity—by accepting the authority of the source of the information, by critical reflection, or by experimentation in practice.

Thus it can be seen that while research reports are valuable contributions to our understanding of the nature of practice and practitioners' own theories of practice, they do not provide a perfect reflection of either. Indeed, they might be regarded as information rather than as knowledge—a distinction to which we will return.

Since the reports might be incorporated into the bodies of knowledge of certain professions and because they are also built into the theory of the professions by way of inclusion in the curricula of professional preparation, their limitations as well as their strengths need to be acknowledged. In addition, these limitations need to be taken into consideration when practitioner-researchers are undertaking research at the behest of management, so that management can endeavor to make decisions and predict results in a "scientific" manner. The information provided may well be extremely useful and provide additional insights into situations where decisions have to be made or policy is to be formulated, but they do not provide infallible data, no matter how good the research. Consequently, policy decisions are not necessarily going to produce the best outcomes simply because they are based on research. To think otherwise is to accept the very technical rationality that Schön (1983) did so much to undermine.

The limitations of research acknowledged here do not mean that we should not welcome its continued growth or the expansion of the numbers of practitioners who have become practitioner-researchers. They do, however, point to the fact that uncritical awareness of the limitations of research can result in wrong decisions, bad policy, or misunderstanding about the nature of the social reality being investigated. It can also mean that the teaching of research-based theory has to recognize the same limitations, meaning that, for instance, it is wrong to assume that such theory can be automatically and uncritically applied to practice.

The more research that is undertaken by practitioner-researchers, the more information we will have about the processes of practice, the development of practical knowledge, and other relevant facets among practitioners. This can only augur well for our understanding, provided that no attempts are made to prescribe practice by reports of past practice rather than recognize the uniqueness of the present and encourage innovative practice based on inductive reasoning and the expertise of the practitioners.

Conclusion

This discussion has considerable implications for a great number of things, including the nature of theory, the relationship between theory and practice, the validity and assessment of professional knowledge, the role of universities and professional schools in the training and examining of new recruits to professions and occupations, the provision of continuing education, the place of universities as research institutions, the nature of research itself, and the relationship between universities and practice. Each of these points might constitute a book in itself, but we will begin to explore some of them in the remaining chapters, with special reference to the emergence of practitioner-researchers and the research they undertake.

Chapter Thirteen

Theory Reconceptualized

In Chapter Twelve, we discussed the idea that practitioners develop their own theory of action; I called this idea both *personal theory* and *practical knowledge*—I use the terms interchangeably. I have also pointed out that when practitioner-researchers publish the results of their research, the contents sometimes get included in professional schools' curricula and in professions' bodies of knowledge—and in each case they are referred to as theory. It was suggested in Chapter Twelve, however, that these published reports contain information to be learned. Only when the information is learned can it become knowledge. But that knowledge is legitimated for the practitioners only when it is tried out in practice and found to work. Then it becomes part of the personal theory. We therefore have three totally different concepts here:

- Personal theory/practical knowledge: validated by successful practice
- Information: to be communicated to others
- Knowledge: information learned but not yet validated by successful practice

We also see the terms *knowledge* and *theory* being used in different ways; in a sense there is a degree of ambiguity in the way they are used.

In a similar manner, Argyris and Schön ([1974] 1992) were forced to distinguish between their theories of action: they used the terms *espoused theory* and *theory in use*. The latter term relates fairly closely to the idea of personal theory or practical knowledge used here, although the idea of an espoused theory might refer to a set of values, an occupational ideology, or merely what was learned in university or professional training school in initial professional preparation.

This chapter provides a framework within which we can reconceptualize the term *theory* and show that there are a variety of concepts in everyday use, four of them important to our understanding of the foregoing discussion. The chapter has two main parts: the first examines how theory has been defined in the past, and the second reconceptualizes it in the light of the discussion throughout this book.

Meanings of the Term *Theory*

An early dictionary of sociology (Mitchell, 1968) contains the following description of the term *theory*:

> The term *theory* is one of the most misused and misleading terms in the vocabulary of the social scientist. It may refer to an abstract conceptual scheme which in itself may be little more than a number of definitions, or it may be systematic reference so that each abstract term is systematically related to the others, rendering the categories exclusive to each other, but pointing to their articulation. If, from such a categorical system, laws may be derived possessing predictive value, then we may say that a *theoretical* system has been evolved. Strictly speaking only this last kind of system is a system of theory, and a law, or generalisation derived from it, is properly called a *theory*. There is a very loose use of the term *theory* to mean that part of the study of a subject which is not practical. In the training of social workers *theory* is often contrasted with *practical work*, but what is meant here is merely the more academic aspects of a course of instruction [p. 228].

This quotation indicates how social scientists regarded the term at a time, in the 1960s, when sociology was trying to emulate the sciences. For them, theoretical systems were a form of law, having predictive value. We have already noted, however, that the research conducted by practitioner-researchers is about unique and unrepeatable events—that their reports record historical happenings, past events. Because the events are unique, they cannot be replicated in precisely the same way, so the emphasis on laws having predictive value no longer rings true. Indeed, we might go so far as to claim that laws might inhibit the art of practice, so we reject the idea of theory being about laws that have predictive value. Even so, we recognize that because of the process of habituation and the idea of habitus, there are similarities in practice, so theoretical understandings of past events might allow us to hypothesize about future actions.

In contrast, in the comments about the training of social workers, theory means only that it is academic as opposed to practical and that the academic consequently defines the practice for practitioners who are involved in nonacademic practical work. This distinction is no longer acceptable to practitioner-researchers who endeavor to practice in a reflective manner or who also research their own practice.

Even so, it does reflect one idea that has been implicit in a great deal of the discussion throughout this book but has not yet been discussed. The research of practitioner-researchers produces integrated information about practice, but there is occasional research from researchers who stand outside of practice and study it from the perspective of an academic discipline, meaning that we can have a sociology of education, a psychology of interpersonal behavior, and so on. There are also scholars who "theorize" about fields of practice from their own discipline perspective, thus constituting fields of study or academic subdisciplines. This is a form of theoretical knowledge, distinct from practical knowledge and driven by the internal logic of the discipline concerned. Understanding social work from a sociological or philosophical perspective has also constituted part of this body of theory. Theory is often granted high status because it comes from the perspectives of established academic disciplines. This is what I referred to in Chapter Twelve as metatheory.

Nevertheless, it is easy to see why occupations and professions have placed such high value on theory, especially of the metatheoretical kind, and why research was regarded as the preserve of the academics, since they needed to have mastery of one of the traditional disciplines. The high status accorded to theory is something that the work of practitioner-researchers is beginning to undermine. Now the idea that practice, or social phenomena of any kind, consists of social facts is totally unacceptable; even the idea that theory is an explanation of those facts is itself no longer acceptable, seeing that research reports are necessarily social constructs.

Indeed, all explanations are social constructions, and Geuss (1981), for instance, has suggested that "a social theory is a theory *about* . . . agents' beliefs about their society, but it is *itself* such a belief" (p. 56). In other words, the critical theorists and others regard theories as explanatory frameworks that are themselves belief systems that need to be deconstructed to discover what lies behind them—if anything. Even the academic disciplines are not exempt from this analysis; their interpretations are themselves ideological. They are part of the discourse about social phenomena and have become incorporated into professional curricula, as Foucault (1972) has claimed (see also Sheridan, 1980). In his thinking, discourse is a reflection of the power of those engaged in constructing the discourse: the theorists, who spoke on behalf of the practitioners and the profession or occupation as a whole and whose discourse also defined practice. This is no longer the case; now practitioner-researchers speak about their practice and largely determine how it should be performed.

Theory, then, can no longer be regarded as value-free, even though it might contain attempts to state a "truth" as it is perceived by the individuals engaged in the discourse. But it is not usually the practitioners telling their story. Mitchell's definition (1968) suggested that this discourse was merely the academic element of a course of instruction, which was itself rather a sweeping claim.

More recently, Outhwaite (1983) suggested that theory is a

> body of law-like generalizations, logically linked to one another, which can be used to EXPLAIN empirical phenomena . . . But, as has been stressed by "linguistic" philosophers of science, most theories are not as neat as their idealized representations in text-books. In the social sciences the term "theory" is used very loosely, and may mean no more than a set of assumptions or concepts, or a relatively abstract inquiry distinguished from empirical research or practical recommendations [p. 395].

Outhwaite's definition recognizes that all the social sciences' bodies of knowledge are much looser than those of the physical sciences. He goes on to point out that those theories contained in textbooks are constructs in order to make them "logically neat"; that is, their coherency is provided by the textbook authors, which does not reflect the fragmentation of practice itself. In other words, it is the authors' *discourse* about practice, an attempt to define practice for their readers and students.

But practice is complex, and all the research reports are no more than representations of unique transitory events. To try to build these reports into a coherent body of knowledge may be a useful heuristic exercise, but it does not provide a good reflection of practice, not does it ring true to our understanding of the way that practitioner-researchers undertake their research and produce their reports.

Without seeking further definitions of the concept of theory, we can see that scholars have recognized that it is a construction and that their discussions indicate that the term is no more than a broad "umbrella-like" concept to which it is almost impossible to give a single definition. The question we must now confront is this: Should we try to offer a single definition at all? In everyday speech, the term has at least five different meanings (*Collins English Dictionary,* 1979):

A plan formulated in the mind

A system of rules, procedures, and assumptions

Abstract knowledge or reasoning

A set of hypotheses

A hypothesis (in nontechnical usage)

Consequently, we can see that it would be difficult, if not impossible, to provide a single definition that covers every conceivable use of the term. The only things we can claim are that theories are contrasted to practice in some way since they are cognitive or informational. Even then, we have to note that they are constructs that do not provide a complete representation of whatever reality, if any, lies behind them.

We are now in a position to try to reconceptualize theory from within the framework of our discussion on practitioner-researchers.

Theory Reconceptualized

It is clear from the foregoing that it is no longer possible to treat theory as a coherent entity that can be generalized to all practice situations. Indeed, it is questionable whether the high status of theory should be retained in its present form in light of the current emphasis on practice, reflective practice, practical knowledge, and practitioner-researchers' research into practice. Practical knowledge, however, might be regarded as a new aspect of theory, a personal theory of practice.

Information about practice exists in two quite distinct forms. The first is the integrated knowledge of practice, which stems from research into practice conducted by practitioner-researchers—educational knowledge, consultancy knowledge, nursing knowledge, and the like. The second stems from the disciplines, either as unitary or multidisciplinary knowledge about practice. We have also distinguished between knowledge, which is learned and is subjective, and information, which is potential knowledge to be learned and is objective.

There are therefore four distinct formulations that can now be called theory:

- *Personal theory of practice* (theory as knowledge)—practical knowledge, including both process and content
- *Theory of practice* (theory as information)—a combination of both integrated knowledge of the process and content knowledge; both become integrated into personal theory when they have been tried and found to work in practice
- *Theory about practice* (metatheory as information)—based in the academic disciplines and making few claims of practicality
- *Theory of and about practice* (knowledge learned but not tried out in practice)—learned cognitively from both forms of information

Let us look at each of these definitions in turn.

Personal Theory of Practice

Knowledge learned in practice is flexible and driven by the demands of practice, although there are times when practitioners do not respond to the learning opportunities provided by practice and so do not always adapt their knowledge base to its exigencies and learn from disjunctural situations and critical incidents. Personal theory consists of fully integrated knowledge that combines learning from doing and thinking about practice with learning from other information sources, such as content knowledge learned from metatheory. It is therefore pragmatic, although the outcomes themselves are social constructs (see Chapter Twelve).

Theory of Practice

This is part of the professional curriculum or body of knowledge, provided to new entrants to a profession or occupation, and it may also form part of a continuing education or staff development curriculum. It comes mainly from research reports, policy statements, and similar sources. Some of this information is contained in the research reports produced by practitioner-researchers, especially educators who are able to use their own research in teaching. Otherwise, the practitioner-researchers' work gets used only if it is published.

Theory About Practice

As explained in Chapter Twelve and earlier in this chapter, what I call metatheory is also part of the professional curriculum and body of knowledge. It is information stemming from the academic disciplines and driven by the internal logic of the discipline rather than by the exigencies of practice.

There are two elements to metatheory. The first is the content knowledge for practice, learned by studying the academic disciplines that underlie practice. For instance, it is important for a doctor to have a knowledge of anatomy, a policeman to know the law, and so on. Then there is the knowledge about the profession or occupation, based in academic disciplines such as sociology, philosophy, and economics. The latter makes no pretense of being applicable to practice, but it tends to contextualize it. The learning is cognitive, but it may be useful information when the practice as a whole is in the spotlight. For instance, having sociological and economic information about providing education for older adults might well affect policy decisions, and understanding the cost benefits of community care might affect policy decisions on health care.

It might be argued that since metatheory is not directly applicable to practice, it is not all relevant to practitioners. Practitioners whose priority is immediate relevancy will be primarily interested in content knowledge, but this does not mean that the knowledge about practice should not be available to them or that they should not be given other intellectual tools to understand metatheoretical formulations about their work.

Theory of and About Practice

This is knowledge gained as a result of learning in the cognitive domain. It has not been tested in practice, so in a sense it remains "merely academic." Its legitimacy lies in the authority of the source of the information, in the internal logic of the information, or in acceptance of the information as a result of reflective learning. In a sense, this is what is learned in the professional curriculum before new recruits become practitioners.

Conclusion

In this chapter, we have reconceptualized theory. A fundamental distinction is drawn between knowledge, or what has been learned by individuals, and information, or what is contained in reports and might be learned and become knowledge. This distinction has not been made a great deal in the past, but it is considered useful now in our information society. Information comes from a variety of sources, and in our learning, its validity is tested through critical thinking (Brookfield, 1987). What is learned and accepted then becomes knowledge. Knowledge is subjective; information is not. But one person's knowledge becomes another's information. Hence the practitioner-researchers' reports are their knowledge but the readers' information.

We have also highlighted the fact that practical knowledge is integrated knowledge driven by the demands of practice, whereas information about practice is often based in a single academic discipline and driven by the demands of that discipline. These two forms of knowledge are fundamentally different, therefore, and have to be treated differently in discussions about theory.

The theory taught in professional schools and universities is information for the learners; until they have tested it out, it does not become practical knowledge. A great deal of practical knowledge, however, is learned by practitioners in practice that is not contained in reports. In other words, knowledge that has never actually been information may never find its way into bodies of knowledge or professional schools' curricula.

The following chapter expands the discussion of the relationship between theory and practice conducted in this chapter and Chapter Twelve by questioning the traditional formulation that theory should be applied to practice.

Chapter Fourteen

From Practice to Theory?

As we have seen throughout this book, and especially in Chapter Twelve (Figure 12.1), the old idea that theory should be applied to practice is hardly tenable now. We saw how practitioners produce their own personal theory as a result of reflecting on their own work situations and learning from their experiences. We also showed that metatheory (in the form of continuing learning), which is information, feeds into the learning and reflection process, which in turn only becomes part of personal theory after it has been tested out in the practice situation and found to be successful. In these situations, therefore, we can claim that practice precedes personal theory, the dynamic personal theory then guides future practice, and so on in a continuous cycle.

Two further questions about this relationship, however, still require further exploration: What is the sequence for initial professional preparation? And what is the relationship among practice, research, and theory? Let us examine these questions one at a time.

Initial Professional Preparation

It is essential to reiterate that the content of professional schools' curricula and the bodies of knowledge of occupations and professions constitute *information* for new recruits—representations of social phenomena, not knowledge. Learners have the opportunity to learn that information, recognizing that it comes from two distinct sources that are driven by different logics and demands. It is important to highlight to learners that the theory of practice and the theory about practice are completely different: the former is integrated, and the latter is discipline-based. Unfortunately, the integrated theory of practice—educational knowledge, nursing knowledge, and so on— is often presented to students as if it were the same as the discipline-based information. But it is not: the one is driven by the demands of practice and the other by the internal logic of the discipline. It is possible, for instance, to have a sociology of medical practice or a philosophy of management, but it is not possible to have a management of philosophy or a medical practice of sociology. There is a profound difference between the two, and this is why I have differentiated them here as personal theory and metatheory.

Making this distinction clear to students from the outset is very important in the learning process because the validity of the information can only be critically assessed from within the framework of its construction. It is no good, for instance, rejecting sociological theories of education because they will not work in practice, for they are never intended to work in practice. The criteria for criticality need to be outlined specifically for the learners. As they study the information, some of it will be learned and will then become unvalidated knowledge for them, while other information will either not be considered or be rejected for a variety of reasons.

It is only in the internship situation, and in practice thereafter, that the new recruits can test out that knowledge and see whether it is practical, or relevant in the case of some of the metatheory, to their practice. Only then does it become incorporated into the body of personal theory and we can then see how the process described in Figure 12.1 develops from there. Figure 14.1 records the process we have described so far in this chapter.

In this instance, we see the tenuous relationship between theory as information and practice, and we also see that the learning processes of new recruits is incomplete until they have the opportunity to practice what they have learned. We can trace this process in the following manner:

1. The new recruits are provided with information.

Figure 14.1. Relationship Between Theory and Practice for New Recruits.

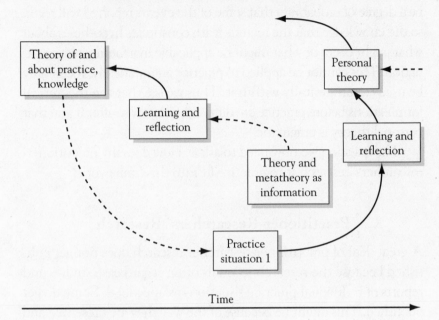

Time

Note: Dotted lines indicate weaker links than solid lines.

2. They learn the information, which becomes theory (knowledge about practice) for them.

3. They try it out in practice.

4. They reflect on their experiences.

5. They generate their own personal theory.

6. The loop continues as in Figure 12.1.

Consequently, there have been many experiments in recent years to change the structure of initial preparation of recruits so that the new entrants to an occupation or profession have the opportunity to undertake more practice during this initial preparation period.

It is also important to recall that the information presented to new recruits is historical, albeit often very recent, frequently reporting transitory and ephemeral events of practice. Consequently, it cannot legitimately be claimed that this information can be applied to future practice. What can be claimed, however, is that there might be a degree of probability that some of the events reported will recur, so the knowledge that the recruits learn constitutes hypotheses about what might occur or what might be applicable in a future practice situation. This cannot be applied to practice automatically; it can only be used experimentally within it. Thus we see that the theoretical formulations before practice are different from those after it and that personal theory is pragmatic.

The question we now need to ask is, How does the practitioner-researchers' research into practice fit into this framework?

Practitioner-Researchers' Research

A great deal of practitioner-researcher research does not get published because the research journals often regard case studies and reports of individual practice situations as anecdotal. Some do get published. This might be because of the way they are presented and argued from an academic perspective. At the same time, more practitioner-researcher reports do get published in practitioner journals, and they then provide information for other practitioners to use.

As noted, some research reports are commissioned by management to help in decision making. I have argued in this book that such information reports on historical and transitory events, and thus that it constitutes only hypotheses for the future. I have also pointed out that these reports are themselves social constructs rather than accurate scientific analyses of empirical facts. Consequently, such reports in themselves do not provide the basis for scientific management decisions; all they can provide is information to assist in the decision-making process. To treat such reports as if they can provide the bases for decision making is to create a technical-rational situation, which Schön (1983) rightly declared of dubious value in many practice situations. We have to make certain that scientific management does not seek to reinvent an outdated and discredited wheel.

How, then, does the practitioner-researchers' research relate to our discussion here of theory and practice? Figure 14.2 depicts the process.

Once again we have a loop, but this time it is more complicated. In this instance, we see the following:

1. The first practice assumes that the practitioner has received some theory as information, as seen in Figure 14.1.

2. The first practice is researched and the results are either incorporated into the theory as information or interpreted by the academic disciplines and become a part of metatheoretical formulation.

Figure 14.2. Theory, Practice, and Research.

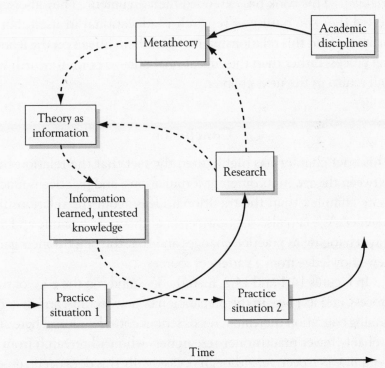

Note: Dotted lines indicate weaker links than solid lines.

3. The metatheoretical formulation might then be incorporated into the theory as information.

4. The theory as information is learned, but it is untested.

5. The learning constitutes hypotheses for new practice by practitioners.

6. The practitioners' learning is tested, and the new knowledge is incorporated into their personal theories or rejected as not being practical or relevant.

7. The loop continues as in Figure 12.1, or the new practice can be researched and the loop then continues.

Usher and Bryant (1989), in their very important book about research, theory, and practice, have argued that the relationship between adult education as practice, theory, and research is a "captive triangle." This book has extended their argument. They also suggested that the nature of research is educational in itself, but I maintain that this relationship between them hinges on the learning process rather than the educational one—a point to which we will return in the next chapter.

Conclusion

This brief chapter has highlighted the fact that the relationship between theory, in its different formulations, and practice is much more complex than the traditional ideas about the relationship assumed. We can also see how personal theory is dynamic and always changing as practice changes and that the practitioners gain new knowledge from a variety of sources.

In Figures 14.1 and 14.2, metatheory stands on the edge of the process, and its place in the preparation of new recruits, and in continuing education thereafter, needs serious consideration. There are probably fewer practitioner-researchers who will research from a discipline perspective, although occasionally this does occur, especially if a practitioner-researcher has studied a particular discipline prior to entering the occupation or profession. It is, however, unwise to attempt to research from the perspective of an academic discipline without having a thorough grounding in it. For instance, having studied one or two modules in a foundation program is certainly insufficient to claim to understand the intricacies of an academic discipline such as sociology or philosophy. Indeed, the claim from a particular discipline perspective without having a considerable level of knowledge of that discipline discredits practitioner research in the eyes of discipline-oriented scholars. Consequently, practitioner-researchers should seek collaborative research projects with specialists from the disciplines if they feel that this type of interpretation would enrich their research.

Although research throws considerable light on the practice situation, it does not constitute an infallible guide either to decision making or to practice. We return to the nature of research in the following chapter.

Part Five

Reflections on the Practitioner-Researcher

Chapter Fifteen

Practitioner Research and the Learning Society

Throughout this book, there has been a recognized interrelationship between research and learning; indeed, in Chapter Eight especially we noted how reflective learning and action research became almost interchangeable concepts at one point. Consequently, the relationship between the practitioner-researchers' research and the learning that occurs in practice does require some exploration. In this chapter we undertake this journey and explore the idea that the emergence of practitioner-researchers is a symbol of the development of the learning society. The chapter has five sections: the first briefly explores the idea of the learning society, the second analyzes the relationship between research and learning, the third examines the emergence of practitioner-researchers in the learning society, the fourth looks at the process of democratizing research, and the fifth explores the relationship among learning, research, and scholarship.

The Idea of the Learning Society

The learning society is a metaphor to describe the type of society in which we live, and here I want to examine three different interpretations of it: as a futuristic and a rather idealistic concept, as a learning market, and as a reflexive society. I want to show how this book's argument reflects the fact that we do live and practice in a learning society of a reflexive nature, although some of the ideas from the first two interpretations are also relevant to our discussion.

The Learning Society as Futuristic

When Hutchins (1968) wrote his classic book on the learning society, he looked to the future and suggested that the learning society "would be one that, in addition to offering part-time adult education to every man and woman at every stage of grown-up life, had succeeded in transforming its values in such a way that learning, fulfilment, becoming human, had become its aims and all its institutions were directed to this end" (p. 133). For Hutchins, education would come into its own, and the new learning society would be the building of a new Athens, made possible not by slavery but by modern machines. It was the realization of the computer revolution that led Husen (1974) to very similar conclusions. He argued that "*educated ability* will be democracy's replacement for passed-on social prerogatives" (p. 238). This is something to which we will return later in this chapter. He thought that the knowledge explosion would be fostered by a combination of computers and reprographics, and he foresaw the possibility of "*equal opportunities* for all to receive as much education as they are thought capable of absorbing" (p. 240).

More recently, a similar position has been adopted by Ranson (1994), who has suggested that "there is a need for the creation of a learning society as the constitutive condition of a new moral and political order. It is only when the values and processes of learning are placed at the centre of the polity that the conditions can be established for all individuals to develop their capacities, and that institutions can respond openly and imaginatively to a period of change" (p. 106). Ranson approached the subject starting with school education rather than with an adult or lifelong education framework. It is futuristic and rather idealistic. Boshier (1980), while still looking forward to a learning society, actually started from the position of an adult educator and recognized that this new society is about more than school education. He explored the post-school institutions in New Zealand to discover the structural basis of such a society—but it was still an educational phenomenon.

In a sense, each of the theorists discussed here foresaw an educative society. Significantly, all these theorists start their analyses with one part of the public institution, and for them the learning society remains an ideal that will be realized only when the more public institution of education has been reformed. What we have seen in the emergence of the practitioner-researcher has been that a great deal of the learning and the research is practice-based, and so far we have made little reference to the educational institutions.

The Learning Society as a Learning Market

Contemporary society is also a consumer society, and the history of consumerism can be traced back to the eighteenth century (Campbell, 1987). Any analysis of the market requires consumers. Clearly there can be no market economy unless there are consumers who want to purchase the products that are being produced. Advertising plays on imaginary pleasure—and shopping can be fun. Now, as Usher and Edwards (1994) point out, one of the features of contemporary society is that of experiencing—it is a sensate society. This is not new, as Campbell has shown, but it is the type of society in which the longings of the imagination can be satisfied through consumption, and the basis of advertising is thus the cultivation of desire.

When learning is equated with education in people's minds, they tend to remember unpleasant experiences at school, when it might not have been fun to learn, and this can cause them to erect a barrier to further education—a barrier that every adult educator has sought to overcome. But now that learning has become separated from education in many people's minds, learning can become fun. Now people can read books, watch television, listen to the radio, surf the World Wide Web, work on their personal computers, discuss with other people through electronic mail, and acquire and exchange information in many other enjoyable ways. Today it is possible to learn all the things people have ever wanted to know by attending learning groups, using multimedia personal computers and the Internet, and so on. But the providers of these learning materials are now not all educational institutions, and educational institutions are having to change their approach rapidly to keep abreast with a market generating information about all aspects of life every minute of the day. People can now choose the medium they are going to employ to receive their information. There are no age limits. Knowledge production has become an industry, cultivating the desire of people to learn so they can take part in contemporary society. This is now a fundamental motivator behind advertising campaigns.

The information society is a market for information. Providers are manufacturing and selling a wide variety of learning materials. This has created a paradoxical situation: although learning is a private and individual process, one of the features of the market is that the consumption of learning has to be public—conspicuous consumption. Educational institutions make public this private activity; it is part of their institutional business. They grant credit for learning from life experience and thus bring this private learning into the pseudo-public sphere of education (Jarvis, 1996). Because educational qualifications are important for practitioners seeking career advancement, they are engaging in additional study to gain credit. This in turn means that the private learning they formerly undertook to improve their practice for themselves and their clients is now becoming the action research project that constitutes part of their continuing education.

Driven by the desire of producers to provide a learning commodity that can be purchased and by educational institutions that can grant credit for private learning, the learning society as an information market has inadvertently fueled the increase in practitioner-researchers because practitioners need these qualifications for career advancement.

The Learning Society as a Reflexive Society

Reflective learning and reflective practice have become commonplace ideas since Schön (1983). But reflective learning is itself a sign of the times; underlying it is the idea of reflexive modernity, which we briefly mentioned at the start of this book. Giddens (1990) and others have argued that reflexivity is fundamental to the nature of modernity, which overrode all forms of tradition. Giddens wrote:

> The reflexivity of modern social life consists in the fact that social practices are constantly examined and reformed in the light of in-coming information about those very practices, thus constitutively altering their character. We should be clear about the nature of this phenomenon. All forms of a social life are partly constituted by actors' knowledge of those forms. Knowing "how to go on" . . . is in-trinsic to the conventions which are drawn upon and reproduced in human activity. In all cultures, social practices are routinely altered in the light of ongoing discoveries which feed into them. But only in the era of modernity is the revision of convention radicalised to apply (in principle) to all aspects of human life [pp. 38–39].

Society has become reflexive, and the knowledge that people acquire is no longer certain and established forever—its value lies in its enabling them to live in this rapidly changing society. The pace of change is now so rapid that everybody is required to learn new things regularly just to keep up. Much of this learning is indi-vidual and private, but some of it is more public. This is very clearly the case with the knowledge-based occupations, as we have seen. For instance, practitioners are required to keep abreast with the changes occurring within their occupational field. Hence there has been a mushrooming of vocational qualifications, especially at the advanced-degree level. This tremendous growth in new informa-tion and the very rapid changes that are occurring in society reflect the idea that the learning society is intrinsic to modernity.

From the perspective of rapidly changing knowledge, there is a fundamental shift in the conception of knowledge itself, from some-thing that is certain and true to something that is fluid and relative. Underlying this form of society is experimentation, which itself leads people to reflect continually on their situation and on the knowledge they possess to cope with it. The need to learn new knowledge is pervasive, but learning new things and acting on them always contains an element of risk. Paradoxically, learning is also a reaction to risk—the risk of not always knowing how to act in this rapidly changing world. Reflexivity is a feature of modernity (Beck, 1992). Reflective learning is a way of life rather than a discovery made by educators and something to be taught in educational institutions. The learning society, then, according to this interpretation, is not a hope for the future but an ever-present phenomenon of the contemporary world. This is the very same case made in our discussion of the uniqueness and transitory nature of practice: reflective learning in practice is a symbol of the learning society.

Learning and Research

The reflexive society is a rapidly changing one; practitioners cannot always presume upon their practice situations, so they sometimes face disjuncture. Disjunctural experiences are often ones in which individuals ask why or how. These are the questions that commence the learning process; unsurprisingly, they are also the questions that commence the research process.

Cohen and Mannion (1985) made the point that there are three ways by which humans seek the truth: experience, reasoning, and research. I have suggested that learning is the process of creating and transforming experiences into knowledge, skills, attitudes, values, emotions, beliefs, and the senses: indeed, reasoning might also be such a process. Research is also a process of transforming experience, sometimes through a reasoning process, but often through much more controlled methods and techniques. Indeed, it is a process of learning—it is a form of learning, but it is not so broad as learning itself. Research has, as I argued in Part Three, rigorous methods of discovering and analyzing data. It is a restricted form of learning employing these methods. Even so, it is still learning.

We can go further and suggest that the methods we discussed in Part Three are those that enable us to get as close as possible to understanding the unique and transitory nature of the experiences of the practitioners, so that these forms of research reflect the reflexive society. The research I have described in this book is therefore a phenomenon that we might well expect to occur in the learning society. Research itself is intrinsic to the learning society.

Practitioner-Researchers and the Learning Society

Practitioner-researchers, as we have argued, are a new breed of practitioner. They have emerged at this time because practice is changing rapidly, and we can no longer assume that research conducted in the past is replicable in the future. In addition, because knowledge is now relative and changing rapidly, it is essential for knowledge-based workers to keep pace with these changes and to continue their education. Nearly every master's degree requires producing a research dissertation, which has helped to generate more practitioner-researchers.

All of these phenomena are characteristics of reflexive modernity; they are all part of the learning society. Thus we can claim that the emergence of the practitioner-researcher role is a symbol of both late modernity and of the learning society in its reflexive form.

Democratization of Research

Research has traditionally been associated with the empirical and the scientific, a realm of high-status knowledge, and researchers were automatically treated as people from the upper echelons of the learned society. Indeed, this high status is reflected in the fact that, as McNiff (1988) has rightly claimed, "the epistemology of the empiricist tradition is that theory determines practice. Teachers are encouraged to fit their practice into a stated theory " (p. 13). But this perspective has now been called into question; we have seen that not all theory need relate to practice, and theory that does has the value only of hypothesis rather than of determination. Consequently, the function of control and its associated high status has been undermined. Neither research nor the researchers can now be distanced from everyday practice and ordinary practitioners, as they were in the past. Indeed, practitioner-researchers have broken down the boundaries.

The boundaries of society have become more open; more people can penetrate the apparent mysteries of "scientific" research, and research itself has become much more a part of everyday practice. Lyotard (1984) makes a similar point about education as a whole: "The transmission of knowledge is no longer designed to train an elite capable of guiding a nation towards its emancipation, but to supply a system of players capable of acceptably fulfilling their roles at the pragmatic posts required by its institutions" (p. 48). This is precisely the point I have made about a great deal of practitioner-researchers' research. It is regarded by managers as an essential tool in providing data for them make their decisions. Research, overall, is now about helping the system, organization, or practice improve its performance—which is precisely what action research claimed. Research, then, is no longer only a function of the elite, by the elite, for the elite. Research has been democratized. Practitioner-researchers are now part of the knowledge workforce—perhaps more than one-third of the workforce (Reich, 1991). The learning society is a "flatter" society with fewer layers in its hierarchy, and although it is not entirely democratic, its openness does at least allow people to cross the boundaries of the social strata. Practitioner-researchers do this, and research itself has become a more democratic phenomenon, the outcomes of which can be used more broadly in society.

Research and Scholarship in the Learning Society

The intellectuals did legislate for what was regarded as correct practice, as McNiff (1988) correctly points out, but now that role has changed (Bauman, 1992). Intellectuals have to find a new role in a society that has displaced them politically with managers and allowed their elite research functions to be appropriated and expanded by practitioner-researchers. Now the scholars comment on society from a distance, or as Bauman so beautifully puts it: "The House of Solomon is now placed in a prosperous suburb, far away from ministerial buildings and military headquarters where it can enjoy in peace, undisturbed, the life of mind complete with a not inconsiderable material comfort" (p. 16). Bauman goes on to point out that "contemporary intellectuals must stick unswervingly to the Western injunction of keeping the poetry of values away from the prose of bureaucratically useful expertise" (pp. 16–17). In other words, scholarship contributes to the metatheory in a world where the "useful expertise" is practical and the practitioner-researchers' research focuses on the pragmatic. It is this type of research that provides the basis of policy decisions in a managerial world.

Such academic scholarship, as we have seen, still serves as an important function in both the preparation and the continuing education of practitioners, but its function is now of a more hermeneutic nature—interpreting the developments of practice, highlighting some of the potential pitfalls, and giving advice to the practitioners, the policymakers, and occasionally the politicians.

Herein lies one of the other significant distinctions between theory and metatheory: theory is knowledge of practice; it provides hypotheses for practice, and in this sense it is practical. Metatheory is knowledge about practice and interpretative, and in this sense cannot, and should not, be applied directly to practice.

Conclusion

Practitioner-researchers and their research are a sign of the times. Practitioner-researchers are an intrinsic part of the learning society, responding to the changes with practical knowledge that enables them to cope with the changes. Their research illustrates that in the learning society, many of the research projects need to be small, local, and practical, producing both a personal theory and information about practice.

Can we say that practitioner-researchers are the successors of the scholars whose learning and research have produced the metatheory and the informed comment on the system? Perhaps it would be incorrect to suggest that practitioner-researchers have actually replaced them, although it would be true to say that some of the scholar's functions have been taken over by practitioner-researchers. Even so, a great deal of practitioner-researchers' work is local and specific; the scholars still take a broader perspective and are still able to place the local and specific into a larger context. Consequently, their role is still important, and it is still necessary for practitioner-researchers to understand metatheory and its functions. Metatheory remains part of the curriculum for initial preparation, but perhaps it has an even greater role in the continuing learning of practitioners.

Clearly, however, the concept of the learning society also involves the providers of learning opportunities, especially the professional schools and universities. In the final two chapters of this book, we explore some of the implications of this discussion for providers of learning.

Chapter Sixteen

Practitioners' Continuing Learning

Practitioners' knowledge and practitioner-researchers' research into practitioners' practice and knowledge have been the main foci of this book. We have examined their initial preparation in Chapter Two, but our discussion has profound implications for their continuing learning, since they are learning incidentally and informally in practice all the time. We can also include in this category occupations such as management, consultancy, and even the professoriate that have no introductory preparation. In these latter cases, the practitioners will almost certainly have professional and academic qualifications, and possibly advanced qualifications, in their initial occupation but not in the one they are currently practicing.

In all of these instances, the practitioners are in practice, learning from their experience every day, as in Figure 12.1, and many of them are progressing along the pathway from novice to expert. Consequently, the content of such formal continuing learning programs needs to be relevant to what they are actually doing and must contain opportunities for testing out ideas and theories. For the sake of convenience, I want to separate the learning that occurs in a natural and self-directed manner in ordinary practice from the more formal, or guided, learning that occurs when practitioners and practitioner-researchers undertake a program of continuing professional education. We can therefore reconstruct Figure 12.1 to relate to their specific situation and to the continuing learning in which they might engage (see Figure 16.1). The two figures differ in three ways: first, the relationship between theory or metatheory as information and learning is strengthened; second, learning now includes

Figure 16.1. The Relationship Between Practice, Continuing Learning, and Personal Theory.

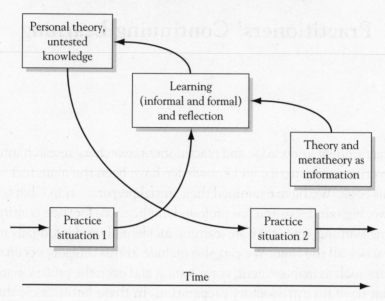

both formal and informal learning; and third, personal theory now includes untested knowledge.

Of course, diagrams like these are heuristic devices intended to demonstrate the process and are necessarily much simpler than the actual process. In this process:

1. The practitioners are in their practice and reflecting on it, as in the normal course of events.

2. The continuing learning is fed into their learning and reflection.

3. They combine their personal theory with untested knowledge.

4. They test their new knowledge in new practice situations.

5. The loop continues with still more new information being fed into their learning, or the loop reverts to the one in Figure 12.1.

In our discussion to this point, we have assumed that the practitioners' learning and research have been driven entirely by the demands of practice. This is the normal process in practice, although because of the demands of continuing professional education, Figure 16.1 depicts a changing reality. We can now see that there are at least two changes in the pattern:

- All the work-based learning is not now totally driven by the demand of practice; some of it will now be guided by the demands of the formal learning.
- Metatheory assumes a greater place in the learning, and this is driven by the demands of the academic discipline.

Preparing a program for continuing learning with experienced practitioners, or their employers, who know what they want for their staff, is now no longer the sole prerogative of academics. As Cervero and Wilson (1994) illustrate, there is now a negotiation of interests between the providers and their two sets of clients, the employers and their experienced practitioners.

There are a number of profound implications in this for the providers of continuing learning for the professions, both at organizational level and at the level of the academics themselves. We focus on the latter in the remainder of this chapter and on the former in the final chapter of this book.

The Role of the Academic

It is clear from the foregoing discussion that, as Bauman (1992) put it, the role of academics has changed: they are no longer at the center of the power structures of society, although they still have a significant place in the preparation and continuing education of practitioners and researchers. Since there have been a number of recent studies of this changing role (Bauman, 1987; Bourdieu, 1988, among others), we need not pursue this theme extensively here, although a number of immediate points deserve mention:

practitioner expertise and its relationship to teaching, the site of learning and the mode of delivery of learning materials, and the aims and objectives of the learning.

Practitioner Expertise and Its Relationship to Teaching

Traditionally, the academics were the legislators of correct knowledge (Bauman, 1987, 1992), but we have already noted that what academics now do is provide information to the practitioners, whose responsibility it is to test out that information and transform what is relevant into their own personal theory, or knowledge. In a sense, information has a lower status than knowledge, which in turn reflects something of the changing status of postcompulsory education, which is no longer an elite activity.

Academics are often not practitioners in the fields they teach, and although they should have highly sophisticated metatheoretical knowledge, they are not the experts in the field of practice—their students are. This means that the academics are in a position to help the practitioners develop their own critical faculties (Brookfield, 1987), to provide and interpret metatheory, and to assist in the development of practitioner-researchers, a point to which we shall return. Many academics also practice or act as consultants in the fields in which they teach, and it as expert practitioners or consultants, rather than as academics, that they may be given more authority by their students and be in a position to be able to advise on what is correct practice.

The teaching function, therefore, should be less didactic and authoritarian and more Socratic and democratic—which is no bad thing, since teaching is about adult relationships.

Site of Teaching and Mode of Delivery

Traditionally, practitioners enrolled in programs of the university or the professional school were seen as the clients of the educational institution and attended classes on the university campus or one of its extramural locations. Some of these traditional assumptions are now beginning to change. Students still enroll in programs and will sometimes come to the university. Both employers and practitioners, however, are more interested in improving practice than in learning sophisticated theoretical ideas that hardly affect practice. This should determine what the program, or curriculum, will contain, but it might also determine how and where it will be delivered.

Work-based and distance learning programs have been mushrooming. Complete programs are now being taught in the workplace, others are being provided in remote locations in both written and electronic form. The workplace is rapidly becoming as significant a site for learning as the campus. As a result, the professoriate's teaching role is changing considerably. Educators might

- Become learning consultants, go to the workplace, and plan formal learning programs with employers and practitioners based in practice itself
- Prepare more study guides and distance learning courses that practitioners can use in their practice
- Become facilitators of learning in the practice situation, rather than didactic teachers providing information to be learned
- Retain their traditional role, although it might not play such a significant part in their teaching in the future as it has in the past

These changes are an illustration of the way in which practice is changing in university teaching, as I indicated about my own role earlier in the book. Throughout the book we have discussed the rapidly changing role of practice, and perhaps these comments provide an excellent illustration of just how rapidly practice is changing. Now the professoriate needs to be trained to be educational consultants, writers of instructional materials, experts in the use of electronic means of communication, facilitators of learning, supervisors of research, and so on.

Aims and Objectives of Learning

Traditionally, academics have been concerned that their students learn the correct knowledge and skills. In continuing professional education, the major objective for many practitioners might be that they improve their practice, that their practice might become more efficient and more effective, and so on. In my own discussions with management consultants recently, they have been asking questions about the "value added" to practice as a result of continuing formal learning. This is not something that has normally concerned academics, but as academia becomes part of the competitive world of industry and commerce, these concerns are becoming more significant. This might mean, therefore, that while we still engage in formative and summative evaluations of our programs, we will need to introduce regular impact evaluations at both the individual practitioner and organizational level.

At the same time, we should not throw the baby out with the bath water. Academics should still be concerned

- About the ability of practitioners to cope with reasoned and critical argument
- That practitioners learn how to learn in a reflective manner
- That students seek after a better understanding of reality than they had before
- That the practitioners who study with them have a good knowledge of some aspects of metatheory and can use it to situate their practice in the wider world
- That the practitioner-researchers they develop become competent researchers

Recognition of the changing role of academia should not mean that the very important human abilities that higher education encourages should not still be fostered and prized both within academic circles and beyond. Indeed, it might well be argued that these abilities are also required in practice.

Practical Knowledge

The emphasis on practical knowledge has implications for continuing learning in a number of ways. We will examine four of them: the accreditation of prior experiential learning, making learning materials relevant to practice, assessing learning, and accrediting programs.

Accreditation of Prior Experiential Learning (APEL)

Universities and colleges have usually treated knowledge in a rather sequential and hierarchical manner. In addition, correct knowledge has been learned and assessed in the academic institution. For instance, it was not possible to enter a university until students had obtained qualifying grades at the high school level, one could not progress to a master's degree until one had obtained a first degree in that subject or to a doctorate without having earned a master's, and so on. This still obtains in many places in the world, and in my own work as a visiting academic in a number of countries in the past few years, I have experienced it on a number of occasions. This assumes, however, the primacy of theory over practice, that academic learning occurs only in academic locations, and that academic learning is recognized by academic qualifications. None of these points are accepted in this book.

People do learn from their experience; this is the basis of the learning diagram shown in Figure 4.1. It is also the foundation of the movement from novice to expert—individuals learn from their experience. Therefore, academic institutions are rightly beginning to try to grant credit for experiential prior learning, even though it has not occurred in a traditional academic framework. But they should do so only on very strict criteria and the ability of the applicants for such credit to argue their cases. Regrettably, some academic institutions of less than the highest standards are accrediting prior experiential learning easily, as if they need to fill their programs, and easy access has become a sales technique in the learning market.

Relevance of Learning Materials

The design of many programs for practitioners has changed considerably. Now there is less emphasis on information to be learned, although information—both theory and metatheory—should be included. There is more emphasis on testing out the information, so much of it has to be relevant to the learner's practice situation. The practitioners might be invited to

- Undertake activities and exercises, using new information based on their own practice position—a form of action research
- Reflect on what they did in specific situations and consider how they solved, or failed to solve, problems they encountered
- Reflect on their attitudes, beliefs, emotions, and so on, in specific practice situations

I have on my desk the draft of a study guide for a distance learning module for a management consultancy master's program, and almost at random I have selected an activity for the learners to undertake. The activity gives the learners, who are practicing management consultants, a piece of information about different styles of collecting and analyzing information. It then asks them to consider which style most reflects their own, whether they can think of situations where their clients expected them to play their role according to a different style, and how they resolved the differences in expectations in the actual practice situation.

These mental skills—being conscious of different ways of collecting information, knowing that clients might have different understandings of how data should be gathered, and being aware of potential interpersonal conflicts and how they might be averted—might all come in handy in future situations the consultants encounter. Even more, seeing that they coped successfully with a potential problem might give these practitioners a good feeling so they can face other interpersonal problems in practice with confidence.

The activity encourages the learners to record their own practical reasoning, so it assists them in the development of their own reflective practice. The author of the study guide is a university professor who is facilitating reflective learning, but he neither controls the learning outcomes nor even knows what they might be. The exercise might be useful to the management consultants studying this module, but for others it might not be of any use at all.

The exercise is grounded in the practitioners' experience. They are asked to learn in one of their own practical situations, and there is no correct response to the learning. If what the students learn is useful to them, the exercise has been good; if it is not useful, they should not pursue it. The information they gain becomes incorporated into their personal theory only after they have tried it out and found that it works for them.

In this example, the whole tenor of the teaching has changed; the practitioners are responsible for their own learning, and they can use the activity in the study guide as they wish. The point is that it is directly oriented to their practice.

Assessing Learning

The pragmatic nature of such practice-based programs causes considerable difficulty with traditional assessment procedures. Pragmatic knowledge is tested in practice and accepted or rejected on the grounds of whether or not it works. A number of questions do arise, for example:

How does one assess a course paper when there are no correct answers?

How can an assessor be sure that the students have sufficient knowledge to be awarded the degree?

How can one be sure that the standard has reached whatever graduate degree level is?

Is something that works in practice necessarily correct?

These are the type of questions that practice-based formal continuing learning instructors confront. Naturally, there are no easy answers. Indeed, it might prove difficult to fail a term paper based on an exercise that has proved useful to the practitioner and has been successful in practice. At the same time, there are still certain academic conventions about standards, such as well-structured logical argument, awareness of similar research and theoretical literature, and clear reporting of the learning that has been achieved. Consequently, academic processes, rather than correct outcomes, are the bases for such decisions.

This does not detract from the assessment process: it has always been subjective, although it has tried to present an objective front. Academic assessors, like any other individuals, construct their own understanding of the papers they read and place their own subjective assessment on them. In both running and participating in assessment workshops for experienced assessors over the years, I have found that we can expect thirty experienced examiners marking copies of the same paper at the same time to differ in their grades by as much as 40 percent. Consequently, we should expect disagreement between academics marking a piece of work; indeed, agreement might mean that the second marker has not engaged in a critical debate with the script in the same way as the first assessor. Reaching an agreed grade is part of the academic's role.

Accrediting Programs

In light of these many difficulties, academic institutions are introducing tighter quality control mechanisms. For instance, the accreditation of programs is becoming much stricter. This is not only because of the problems introduced by practical knowledge but also because it is easier to see the quality of the institutions' teaching material once the learning materials have been produced in a form other than face-to-face teaching. Distance learning materials, programs on the World Wide Web, and the like, are all in the public domain. Consequently, the quality of such programs reflect the level of the school or university, so their production is being much more rigorously controlled.

Practitioner-Researchers

I have claimed throughout this book that practitioner-researchers are a natural outcome of this learning age. Rapid change means that information about practice quickly becomes out of date, and the rapid development of new theories and new knowledge means that practitioners need to undertake continuing formal learning, as well as learn in and from their practice. The continuing formal learning becomes a type of action research as the learners seek to test out the new knowledge they have gained in practice. But also most programs beyond the undergraduate level expect the participants to undertake a small research project. Consequently, research methods frequently form a compulsory part of such programs—practitioners are taught to be researchers and are expected to conduct research in order to gain their advanced qualifications. Practitioner-researchers are a sign of the times.

As we have seen, this has democratized the research process, but academics, besides being researchers, now have roles in preparing practitioner-researchers, supervising their research, and even, on occasion, collaborating with practitioner-researchers on research projects. The more they collaborate with graduate students who are practitioner-researchers, the more they will bridge the gap between academia and the world of work, and the more they will learn about the fields of practice with which they are involved.

Practitioner-researchers do need to continue their formal learning, so higher degree programs—both practitioner and research doctorates—should also be oriented toward part-time research work in practice. This creates difficulties for universities that have residence requirements for higher-level study, but it may be that it reflects an outmoded understanding of education or even one that is in some ways richer and beneficial but too expensive and time-consuming for many practitioner-researchers.

In addition, creating the possibility of joint appointments between the universities and colleges and the fields of practice, so that practitioner-researchers have adjunct positions, means they can be more active in teaching about their own practice, thereby narrowing the gap between academic theory and practice.

Conclusion

In this chapter, we have explored some of the implications for academia of the way society has changed and the way in which practitioner research has emerged. Universities and professional schools should not be ivory towers, and their practices at the levels of teaching and research need to change. The final chapter in the book continues this theme by speculating a little about the direction that higher education needs to take now that the emphases are on pragmatic knowledge, research into practice, and improving the efficiency of practice to compete in a global market.

Chapter Seventeen

The Universities and the World of the Practitioner-Researcher

Practitioner-researchers are practitioners and frequently undertaking work-based research. Yet the image of researchers has been one of outsiders, usually university-based, coming into the world of practice, seeking to understand it, and disseminating the discovered facts to other interested people both within and outside practice. It is almost as if the universities were implying that the world of practice was a foreign domain to them; they need to study it so they can tell others what it is all about. But that image is disappearing, and with it the idea that we can discover empirical facts that can be reported as "truths" to the outside world. Now the ephemeral events of practice are studied from within, and the interpretive reports are recognized as representations of a transient reality.

There are few underlying empirical facts that can be incorporated uncritically into a body of knowledge or a curriculum to be taught and applied to practice. The reports document past events, and even though history never repeats itself, the information contained in them might prove useful in future events—as hypotheses to be tested in the future. Because practitioner-researchers are increasingly providing the information about practice, the image of research is changing—and so too is the image of the universities. No longer are they ivory towers; in response to the pressures of change, they are becoming "learning universities" (Duke, 1992). In this final chapter, I seek to illustrate how these changes are occurring, but I also suggest that universities must endeavor to retain the things they have that will continue to enrich society in the future.

Widening Access

One of the proud traditions in American universities has been that they were formed to improve the standards of practice, and they have consequently had a wider range of students enrolled in their programs than universities in many other parts of the world. Cabal (1993) provided a recent but very traditional formulation of the role of the universities in those parts of the world, in which there was very little reference to the concerns expressed in this book. In North America and parts of Europe, however, there has grown up a new tradition of many different practitioners from a variety of occupations and professions working toward undergraduate degrees, returning to school to do graduate work, and seeking out university professors to assist them in their research. In many other parts of the world, access to universities has been restricted to young adults, often male, drawn from the social elite. Research, where it has been conducted, has been undertaken by university staff on the outside world.

The American model of wider access to universities at both the undergraduate and graduate levels has to be learned by other countries. Access not only must cover a wide spectrum of young adults but should also last a lifetime so that credits toward degrees can be earned during the whole of one's working life, and beyond it in retirement.

Access should take no heed of social class, age, disability, ethnic origin, or gender. If universities are to be institutions of lifelong learning, they must ensure that everybody who can benefit from them is given the opportunity.

This means that the programs have to be structured and presented in such a way that people can study them at work, at home, and in learning centers in the workplace or in the community. New technology is making this increasingly possible, and so the structure of course provision is undergoing change.

Once universities and professional schools have become institutions of lifelong learning, the traditional mainstay of university teaching—undergraduate programs—begins to take its place in the total provision of lifelong education, among a growing number of graduate programs at both master's and doctoral levels.

Providing courses, often of a highly theoretical nature, has often been at the center of university life. Now two changes have to be incorporated into college teaching: many of the programs have to be more oriented toward practice and practical knowledge, and many of the teachers need to be practitioners.

Access, therefore, has to be widened so that individuals with varied skills and knowledge might teach at the university level. Practitioner-researchers, for instance, with graduate degrees might well be given appointments both to teach and to practice. They might be appointed to be professor-practitioners, or as we call them in the United Kingdom, either teacher-practitioners or lecturer-practitioners. They can use their expertise both in teaching and in research while continuing in practice. Indeed, in preparing a new distance learning course for management consultants, I have found that practitioner-researchers do produce teaching and learning materials of a very high caliber, although it did take the university a long time to accept the materials. To its credit, however, since it did so it has supported the initiative to the fullest.

This model of the professions may seem to fly in the face of the idea that professionals are increasingly developing their own specialty areas on a full-time basis. Many of these models of professions (Caplow, 1954; Greenwood, 1959; Wilensky, 1964; and others) represent a previous era, however, and it can well be argued that we need to rediscover the generalist whose activities can span a number of different areas of society. This is certainly true of the way the universities need to develop, as I argue later in this chapter. More adjunct and part-time appointments would encourage recognition that practice is as much a seat of learning as is the university, that work-based learning is "real" learning, and that practitioner research is legitimate research.

Entering Partnerships

As the "corporate classroom" (Eurich, 1985) emerges, the universities have to recognize their alternatives: to ignore them, compete with them, or cooperate with them.

Many of the corporate universities that are emerging do not see themselves as the sole providers of programs for their own employees, nor actually do they see their clientele as being the corporation's employees only. This is certainly the case with the American corporate universities, where graduates of the Rand, Wang, and Arthur D. Little institutes cannot even expect employment in the corporation that trained them (Eurich, 1985, p. 97). Indeed, this is also the case in the United Kingdom, where the British Aerospace Virtual University sees itself providing programs for learners other than British Aerospace employees, and the University of Industry (being initiated by the U. K. government) is being designed for employees of many different companies. True to the practice of outsourcing, these institutions see themselves entering partnerships with other universities and either developing programs collaboratively or using the most appropriate of programs that already exist in the other universities and colleges. Consequently, it will be impossible for the traditional universities in any country to ignore the educational innovations that are currently emerging in the industrial sector.

At the same time, if the traditional universities do ignore these changes, we might get situations like those postulated by Eurich (1985), in which the corporate universities continue to develop their own qualifications and create a competitive learning market in higher education. It will then be difficult for the traditional universities to compete in such a market, when the corporate organizations want the type of practical knowledge on which their success depends and on which their own practitioner-researchers are already doing research.

Many of the new industrial universities do want to collaborate. At the same time, some of the more traditional universities will find collaboration difficult because, among other reasons, they have tended to regard themselves as the authors and legitimators of academic knowledge. Nevertheless, as the boundaries between different sectors of society begin to be penetrated and cooperation is seen to be mutually beneficial, with each sector sharing its expertise with the others, new formations will begin to appear in higher education.

Even so, there are other obstacles to such cooperation, because the industrial universities have a different culture from the traditional ones. Eurich (1985) writes, "Many deterrents to collaboration stem from matters of style and customary routines. If colleges and universities wish more future cooperation with the corporate classroom, they will have to adjust scheduling and curriculum timeframes for more intensive instruction and learn to teach adults more effectively. This can be done by selected professors interested in particular subjects. . . . Part of the problem in cooperative efforts has been a monolithic attitude, an assumption that the whole institution would be forced to change. Why not, for example, think of individuals?" (p. 126).

Even in the mid-1980s, Eurich recognized the significance of electronic means of teaching and now, more than a decade later, the development of new ways of delivering learning materials is much more fully established. But still the traditional universities move so much more slowly than the corporate classroom does—to the frustration of many who seek to cooperate. Since time also costs money, the frustration can also be very costly.

Practitioner-researchers, like lecturer-practitioners, already stand on the bridge between the two worlds, and their existence demonstrates ways in which the collaboration can be enhanced. Collaborative teaching and collaborative research projects will be mutually beneficial.

Retaining the Valued

The corporate universities need curricula that are oriented in a specific direction: toward manufacturing, marketing, running efficient organizations, and so on. Higher education is much broader, so the traditional universities must ensure that what is valued in their traditions is maintained. This includes

- Teaching the humanities and other disciplines that are not regarded as relevant by the corporations (human beings do not live by bread alone)

- Being humanistic organizations—many corporations share this ethos, committed as they are to human resource development
- Continuing to develop academic scholarship and undertaking research in broader areas of social living
- Being involved in service in the local community
- Retaining academic standards of logic, argument, and debate
- Retaining the freedom of speech that allows academics and universities as a whole an independent voice

That the "seat of learning" is being shared does not mean that it is being transferred. The universities still have a vitally important role to play in the future, but they do have to become learning organizations in a learning society and adapt to the social pressures they are experiencing.

Conclusion

Reflexive modernity is an age of learning; it can be no other. Learning, however, is not just a matter of acquiring new knowledge and skills from academic institutions; it is also about researching—not necessarily large "scientific" research projects, but small ongoing pieces of work that help organizations and practitioners keep up with the changes that are occurring.

But this is a practical age when knowledge is legitimated by its performability, and much of the knowledge we learn must be relevant and practical. Researching the practical world of work—whether routine production, service-based industries, knowledge-based industries, or whatever—is a demand to which every organization that wishes to maintain its place in the global market must respond. Practitioner-researchers are already undertaking this, to some degree, but their role must grow and develop in the coming years. Indeed, work-based learning must not be restricted to merely acquiring new knowledge in order to continue to perform an occupational role, for work-based learning also implies work-based research, and this is what practitioner-researchers are already doing. They are a symbol of the learning society in the workplace—and perhaps we should also be looking for them in the community and in the world beyond work. Their number should grow and their role become more significant as the learning society becomes more central to all of our lives, for lifelong learning is not restricted to work-life learning, and the learning society is wider than the work-based learning society.

References

Argyris, C., Putnam, R., and Smith, D. M. *Action Science: Concepts, Methods, and Skills for Research and Intervention*. San Francisco: Jossey-Bass, 1985.

Argyris, C., and Schön, D. A. *Theory in Practice: Increasing Professional Effectiveness*. San Francisco: Jossey Bass, 1992. (Originally published 1974.)

Aristotle. *The Nicomachean Ethics*. Oxford: World's Classics, Oxford University Press, 1991.

Bailey, K. D. *Methods of Social Research*. London: Collier-Macmillan, 1978.

Barrows, H. S., and Tamblyn, R. M. *Problem-Based Learning: An Approach to Medical Education*. New York: Springer, 1980.

Bauman, Z. *Legislators and Interpreters*. Cambridge: Polity Press, 1987.

Bauman, Z. *Intimations of Post-Modernity*. London: Routledge, 1992.

Beck, U. *Risk Society*. London: Sage, 1992.

Beck, U. "The Reinvention of Politics." In U. Beck, A. Giddens, and S. Lash, *Reflexive Modernization*. Cambridge: Polity Press, 1994.

Benner, P. *From Novice to Expert: Excellence and Power in Clinical Nursing Practice*. Menlo Park, Calif.: Addison-Wesley, 1984.

Blaxter, L., Hughes, C., and Tight, M. *How to Research*. Buckingham, England: Open University Press, 1996.

Boshier, R. *Towards a Learning Society*. Vancouver, B.C.: Learning Press, 1980.

Boud, D. (ed.). *Problem-Based Learning in Education for the Professions*. Sydney: Higher Education Research and Development Society of Australia, 1985.

Boud, D., and Feletti, G. (eds.). *The Challenge of Problem-Based Learning*. London: Kogan Page, 1991.

Boud, D., Keogh, R., and Walker, D. *Reflection: Turning Experience into Learning*. London: Kogan Page, 1985.

Bourdieu, P. *Homo Academicus*. Oxford: Blackwell, 1988.

Bourdieu, P. *The Logic of Practice*. Cambridge: Polity Press, 1990.

Bourdieu, P. *The Field of Cultural Production*. Cambridge: Polity Press, 1993.

Brookfield, S. D. *Understanding and Facilitating Adult Learning: A Comprehensive Analysis of Principles and Effective Practices*. San Francisco: Jossey-Bass, 1986.

Brookfield, S. D. *Developing Critical Thinkers: Challenging Adults to Explore Alternative Ways of Thinking and Acting*. San Francisco: Jossey-Bass, 1987.

Cabal, A. *The University as an Institution Today*. Paris: UNESCO, 1993.

Campbell, C. *The Romantic Ethic and the Spirit of Consumerism*. Oxford: Blackwell, 1987.

Campbell, D. *The New Majority*. Edmonton: University of Alberta Press, 1984.

Caplow, T. *The Sociology of Work*. Minneapolis: University of Minnesota Press, 1954.

Carr, W., and Kemmis, S. *Becoming Critical: Education, Knowledge and Action Research*. London: Falmer Press, 1985.

Cervero, R. M., and Wilson, A. L. *Planning Responsibly for Adult Education: A Guide to Negotiating Power and Interests*. San Francisco: Jossey-Bass, 1994.

Chisholm, R. "Theory and Practice: The Point of Contact." In J. Nyiri and B. Smith (eds.), *Practical Knowledge*. London: Croom Helm, 1988.

Cohen, L., and Mannion, L. *Research Methods in Education*. (2nd ed.) London: Croom Helm, 1985.

Collins English Dictionary. London: Collins, 1979.

Concise Oxford Dictionary. Oxford: Oxford University Press, 1996.

Cross, K. P., and Steadman, M. H. *Classroom Research*. San Francisco: Jossey-Bass, 1996.

"Dearth of Engineers Leads BAe to Plan Its Own University." *London Times*, Mar. 12, 1997, p. 6.

Dewey, J. *Democracy and Education*. New York: Free Press, 1916.

Dingwall, R. *The Social Organization of Health Visitor Training*. London: Croom Helm, 1977.

Dreyfus, S. E., and Dreyfus, H. L. "A Five-Stage Model of the Neural Activities Involved in Directed Skill Acquisition." Unpublished report, University of California, Berkeley, 1980.

Duke, C. *The Learning University*. Buckingham, England: Society for Research into Higher Education/Open University Press, 1992.

Edwards, R. *Changing Places?* London: Routledge, 1997.

Eisner, E. *The Art of Educational Evaluation: A Personal View*. Bristol, Pa.: Falmer Press, 1984.

Elliott, P. *The Sociology of Professions*. London: Macmillan, 1972.

Eurich, N. *Corporate Classrooms*. Princeton, N.J.: Carnegie Foundation for the Advancement of Teaching, 1985.

Feigenbaum, E., and McCorduck, P. *The Fifth Generation*. New York: Signet, 1984.

Finch, B. "Developing the Skills for Evidence-Based Practice." *Nurse Education Today*, 1998, 18(1), 46–51.

Flew, A. *A Dictionary of Philosophy*. London: Pan Books, 1979.

Foucault, M. *The Archaeology of Knowledge*. London: Routledge, 1972.

Freire, P. *Cultural Action for Freedom*. Harmondsworth, England: Penguin, 1972.

Gadamer, H. G. *Philosophical Hermeneutics*. Berkeley: University of California Press, 1976.

Gerth, H. H, and Mills, C. W. (eds.). *From Max Weber*. London: Routledge and Kegan Paul, 1948.

Geuss, R. *The Idea of a Critical Theory*. Cambridge: Cambridge University Press, 1981.

Giddens, A. *The Consequences of Modernity*. Cambridge: Polity Press, 1990.

Giddens, A. *Modernity and Self-Identity*. Cambridge: Polity Press, 1991.

Giroux, H. *Border Crossings*. New York: Routledge, 1992.

Goffman, E. *The Presentation of Self in Everyday Life*. Harmondsworth, England: Penguin, 1959.

Goffman, E. *Asylums*. Harmondsworth, England: Penguin, 1961a.

Goffman, E. *Encounters*. Harmondsworth, England: Penguin, 1961b.

Goffman, E. *Frame Analysis*. Harmondsworth, England: Penguin, 1974.

Greenwood, E. "Attributes of a Profession." *Social Work*, 1959, *2*(3), 44–55.

Guba, E. G., and Lincoln, Y. S. *Effective Evaluation: Improving the Usefulness of Evaluation Results Through Responsive and Naturalistic Approaches*. San Francisco: Jossey-Bass, 1981.

Hammersley, M., and Atkinson, P. *Ethnography: Principles in Practice*. London: Tavistock, 1983.

Hargreaves, P., and Jarvis, P. *Handbook of Human Resource Development*. London: Kogan Page, 1998.

Harvey, D. *The Condition of Postmodernity*. Oxford: Blackwell, 1990.

Heidegger, M. *What Is Called Thinking?* New York: HarperCollins, 1968.

Heller, A. *Everyday Life*. London: Routledge and Kegan Paul, 1984.

Heron, J. "Experiential Research Methodology." In P. Reason and J. Rowan (eds.), *Human Inquiry*. Chichester, England: Wiley, 1981.

Husen, T. *The Learning Society*. London: Methuen, 1974.

Hutchins, R. *The Learning Society*. Harmondsworth, England: Penguin, 1968.

Jameson, F. *Postmodernism*. London: Verso, 1991.

Jarvis, P. *Adult Learning in the Social Context*. London: Croom Helm, 1987.

Jarvis, P. *Paradoxes of Learning: On Becoming an Individual in Society*. San Francisco: Jossey-Bass, 1992.

Jarvis, P. "Educating the Adult Educator in an Information Society: The Role of the University." In M. Collins (ed.), *The Canmore Proceedings*. Saskatoon: Educational Foundations/University of Saskatchewan, 1995.

Jarvis, P. "Public Recognition of Lifetime Learning." In *Lifelong Education in Europe*, 1996, *1*(1), 10–17.

Jarvis, P. *Ethics and Education for Adults in Late Modern Society*. Leicester, England: National Institute of Adult Continuing Education, 1997.

Jarvis, P., and Gibson, S. *The Teacher Practitioner in Nursing, Midwifery and Health Visiting*. London: Croom Helm, 1985.

Jarvis, P., and Gibson, S. *The Teacher Practitioner and Mentor in Nursing, Health Visiting, Midwifery and Social Work.* (2nd ed.) Cheltenham, England: Stanley Thornes, 1997.

Kagan, J. "Developmental Studies in Reflection and Analysis." In A. Cashdan and J. Whitehead (eds.), *Personality, Growth and Learning.* London: Longman, 1971.

Kelly, G. A. *A Theory of Personality: The Psychology of Personal Constructs.* New York: Norton, 1963.

Kolb, D. A. *Experiential Learning.* Englewood Cliffs, N.J.: Prentice Hall, 1984.

Kubr, M. *Management Consulting: A Guide to the Profession.* (3rd rev. ed.) Geneva: International Labor Office, 1996.

Lash, S., and Wynne, B. "Introduction." In U. Beck, *Risk Society.* London: Sage, 1992.

Lave, J. *Cognition in Practice.* Cambridge: Cambridge University Press, 1988.

Lave, J., and Wenger, E. *Situated Learning.* Cambridge: Cambridge University Press, 1991.

Lewin, K. "Group Decision Making and Social Change." In T. M. Newcomb and E. L. Hartley (eds.), *Readings in Social Psychology.* Fort Worth, Tex.: Holt, Rinehart and Winston, 1947.

London, M. *Change Agents: New Roles and Innovation Strategies for Human Resource Professionals.* San Francisco: Jossey-Bass, 1988.

Lyotard, J.-F. *The Post-Modern Condition: A Report on Knowledge.* (G. Bennington and B. Massumi, trans.) Manchester, England: Manchester University Press, 1984.

Lyotard, J.-F. *The Post-Modern Explained to Children.* London: Turnaround, 1992.

Mannheim, K. *Ideology and Utopia.* London: Routledge and Kegan Paul, 1936.

Marsick, V., and Watkins, K. E. *Informal and Incidental Learning in the Workplace.* London: Routledge, 1990.

McNiff, J. *Action Research: Principles and Practice.* London: Macmillan, 1988.

Merriam, S. B. *Case Study Research in Education: A Qualitative Approach.* San Francisco: Jossey-Bass, 1988.

Merriam, S. B., and Caffarella, R. S. *Learning in Adulthood: A Comprehensive Guide.* San Francisco: Jossey-Bass, 1991.

Merriam, S. B., and Simpson, E. *A Guide to Research for Educators and Trainers of Adults.* (2nd ed.) Malabar, Florida: Krieger, 1995.

Meyers, C. *Teaching Students to Think Critically: A Guide for Faculty in All Disciplines.* San Francisco: Jossey-Bass, 1986.

Mezirow, J., "How Critical Reflection Triggers Transformative Learning." In Mezirow, J., and Associates, *Fostering Critical Reflection in Adulthood: A Guide to Transformative and Emancipatory Learning.* San Francisco: Jossey-Bass, 1990.

Mitchell, C. D. (ed.). *A New Dictionary of Sociology.* London: Routledge and Kegan Paul, 1968.

Nadler, G., and Hibino, S. *Breakthrough Thinking*. Rocklin, Calif.: Prima, 1994.

Nyiri, J. "Tradition and Practical Knowledge." In J. Nyiri and B. Smith (eds.), *Practical Knowledge*. London: Croom Helm, 1988.

Outhwaite, W. "Theory." In M. Mann (ed.), *Student Encyclopedia of Sociology*. London: Macmillan, 1983.

Peters, J. M. "Reflections on Action Research." In B. A. Quigley and G. W. Kulne (eds.), *Creating Practical Knowledge Through Action Research: Posing Problems, Solving Problems, and Improving Daily Practice*. San Francisco: Jossey-Bass, 1997.

Picardi, E. "Meaning and Rules." In J. Nyiri and B. Smith (eds.), *Practical Knowledge*. London: Croom Helm, 1988.

Polanyi, M. *The Tacit Dimension*. London: Routledge and Kegan Paul, 1967.

Potter, M. *Representing Reality*. London: Sage, 1996.

Ranson, S. *Towards the Learning Society*. London: Cassell, 1994.

Revans, R. *The Origin and Growth of Action Learning*. Bickley, England: Chartwell-Bratt, 1982.

Reich, R. *The Work of Nations: Preparing Ourselves for Twenty-First Century Capitalism*. New York: Simon & Schuster, 1991.

Reinharz, S. "Implementing New Paradigm Research: A Model of Training and Practice." In P. Reason and J. Rowan (eds.), *Human Inquiry*. Chichester, England: Wiley, 1981.

Sadler, P. *Managing Change*. London: Kogan Page, 1995.

Sanford, N. "A Model for Action Research." In P. Reason and J. Rowan (eds.), *Human Inquiry*. Chichester, England: Wiley, 1981.

Scheffler, I. *Conditions of Knowledge*. Chicago: University of Chicago Press, 1965.

Schön, D. A. *The Reflective Practitioner*. New York: Basic Books, 1983.

Schön, D. A. *Educating the Reflective Practitioner: Toward a New Design for Teaching and Learning in the Professions*. San Francisco: Jossey-Bass, 1987.

Schutz, A., and Luckmann, T. *The Structures of the Life-World*. London: Heinemann, 1974.

Schwab, J. "The Practical: A Language for the Curriculum." *School Review*, 1969, 78, 1–23.

Sheridan, M. *Michael Foucault: The Will to Truth*. London: Tavistock, 1980.

Stake, R. E. "Case Studies." In N. K. Denzin and Y. S. Lincoln (eds.), *Handbook of Qualitative Research*. Thousand Oaks, Calif.: Sage, 1994.

Stehr, N. *Knowledge Societies*. London: Sage, 1994.

Stenhouse, L. *An Introduction to Curriculum Research and Development*. London: Heinemann, 1975.

Stikkers, K. (ed.). *Problems of a Sociology of Knowledge by Max Scheler*. London: Routledge and Kegan Paul, 1980.

Titchen, A. "A Case Study of a Patient-Centred Nurse." In K. W. Fulford, S. Ersser, and T. Hope (eds.), *Essential Practice in Patient-Centred Care*. Oxford: Blackwell, 1996.

Tom, A., and Sork, T. "Issues in Collaborative Research." In D. R. Garrison (ed.), *Research Perspectives in Adult Education*. Malabar, Florida: Krieger, 1994.

Torbert, W. R. "Empirical, Behavioural, Theoretical and Attentional Skills Necessary for Collaborative Inquiry." In P. Reason and J. Rowan (eds.), *Humanistic Inquiry*. Chichester, England: Wiley, 1981a.

Torbert, W. R. "Why Educational Research Has Been So Uneducational: The Case for a New Model of Social Science Based on Collaborative Inquiry." In P. Reason and J. Rowan (eds.), *Humanistic Inquiry*. Chichester, England: Wiley, 1981b.

"TTA Is an 'Insult to the Profession.'" *Times Higher Education Supplement*, April 4, 1997, 3.

Usher, R., and Bryant, I. *Adult Education as Theory, Practice, and Research*. London: Routledge, 1989.

Usher, R., and Edwards, R. *Postmodernism and Education*. London: Routledge, 1994.

Van Maanen, J. *Tales of the Field: On Writing Ethnography*. Chicago: University of Chicago Press, 1988.

Watkins, K. E., and Marsick, V. J. *Sculpting the Learning Organization: Lessons in the Art and Science of Systematic Change*. San Francisco: Jossey-Bass, 1993.

Weber, M. *The Theory of Social and Economic Organizations*. New York: Free Press, 1947.

Wilensky, H. L. "The Professionalization of Everyone?" *American Journal of Sociology*, 1964, 70(2), 137–158.

Williams, M., and May, T. *Introduction to the Philosophy of Social Research*. London: University College London, 1996.

Willis, P. *Learning to Labour*. London: Saxon House, 1977.

Wirth, A. *John Dewey as Educator*. New York: Krieger, 1979.

Yakowicz, W. "Coaching: Collegial Learning in Schools." In V. J. Marsick (ed.), *Learning in the Workplace*. London: Croom Helm, 1987.

Index